By Steven Rinella

Meat Eater

American Buffalo

The Scavenger's Guide to Haute Cuisine

Meat Eater

Meat Eater

★

ADVENTURES FROM THE LIFE
OF AN AMERICAN HUNTER

★

Steven Rinella

Spiegel & Grau

New York

Published in the United States by Spiegel & Grau,
an imprint of The Random House Publishing Group,
a division of Random House, Inc., New York.

Spiegel & Grau and design is a registered trademark
of Random House, Inc.

The skewered-trout drawing on page 200 by Mike Houston
is reprinted courtesy of the artist.

Library of Congress Cataloging-in-Publication Data
Rinella, Steven.
Meat eater: a natural history of an American hunter /
Steven Rinella
p. cm.
ISBN 978-0-385-52981-5
eBook ISBN 978-0-679-64528-3
1. Rinella, Steven.   2. Hunters—United States—
Biography.   3. Hunting—United States—
History.   4. Hunting stories, American.   I. Title.
SK17.R56A3 2012
799.29'0092—dc23   2012018129

Printed in the United States of America on acid-free paper

www.spiegelandgrau.com

2 4 6 8 9 7 5 3 1

First Edition

Book design by Donna Sinisgalli

For Matt and Danny,
brothers and best friends

Contents

Meat Eater

CHAPTER ONE

Standing Ground

★

THIS BOOK HAS a hell of a lot going for it, simply because it's a hunting story. That's because hunting stories are the oldest and most widespread form of story on earth. The genre has been around so long, and has such deep roots, that it extends beyond humans. When two wolves meet up, they'll often go through a routine of smelling each other's breath. For a wolf to put his nose to another wolf's mouth is to pose a question: "What happened while you were hunting?" To exhale is to answer: "You can still smell the blood."

Of course, nothing tells a hunting story like a human. Long ago, our ancestors may have told hunting stories in ways that are similar to those of animals today. It's been proposed that the human kiss finds its origins in a mouth-to-mouth greeting similar to that of the modern wolf's. Similarly, it's been proposed that the handshake originated as a way of proving that neither party was concealing a weapon.

But at some point—at least by fifty thousand years ago, though possibly much earlier—we began to tell our hunting stories through the complex languages that are now a hallmark of our species. Linguists and anthropologists theorize that complex language evolved just for this purpose: to coordinate hunting and gathering activities, to categorize an increasingly complex arsenal of hunting tools and weapons, and to convey details about animals and habitat that might be hidden from sight. In short, language came about for the same purposes that I'm engaged in at this very moment.

Granted, these first hunting stories were probably not "stories" at all, at least not in the way we now think of that word. I imagine them more as instructions and descriptions, which is fitting, since the purpose of the vast majority of writing about hunting today is to teach readers how to do something. This "something" can often be quite esoteric. Maybe it's a technique for hunting mallard ducks over flooded corn in Iowa, or maybe it's an explanation of why it's better to sharpen the blade of your skinning knife at an angle of thirteen degrees rather than fifteen. Hunters usually call this kind of information "how-to," and I have read and enjoyed a great many pieces of how-to writing in my life. But while you will find a trove of hunting tips and tricks within this book, this is not intended as how-to material. Instead, you might think of this book as why-to, who-to, and what-to. That is, this book uses the ancient art of the hunting story to answer the questions of why I hunt, who I am as a hunter, and what hunting means to me.

As I ponder the first of those questions—why do I hunt?—two particular moments come to mind. The first took place on a recent spring day when I was hunting turkeys in the Powder River Badlands of southeastern Montana with my brother Matt. Early that morning we left Matt's pack llamas, Timmy and Haggy, tethered near our camp. Matt headed south, and I went into the next valley to the west. Around late morning I started after a tom, or male turkey, that I'd heard gobbling several hundred yards away. I followed the bird for close to an hour, only once catching a glimpse of it. He was walking fast along the edge of a sandstone cliff, maybe about thirty yards higher than me and two hundred yards out. I sat down amid a tangle of fallen timber and used a turkey call to mimic the soft clucks of a hen.

Almost as soon as I did, the tom jumped off the cliff and took flight. He flapped his wings maybe six times and soared right over my head. Turkeys are not graceful fliers; nor are they graceful landers. This one crashed through the limbs of a ponderosa pine and then thudded to the ground on the timbered slope of a deep ravine off to my left. I turned my head in that direction, so that my chin was over my left shoulder. I kept on clucking. I was hopeful that the tom would come to check on the source of the calls, but after a couple of minutes I hadn't seen or heard a thing. I called some more, but still nothing happened.

You have to be very careful about movement and sound when you're hunting turkeys, so I continued to hold dead still even though I hadn't heard or seen the bird since it landed. Maybe about five minutes went by without my ever turning my head away from its position over my left shoulder.

And then something strange happened. Suddenly, someone sighed very loudly just behind my right shoulder. I've had coyotes and bobcats come to my turkey call, but this sigh sounded like that of an annoyed person who was slightly out of breath from running up a hill. My immediate response was to turn my head very quickly in its direction. My chin was just about to begin passing over my right shoulder when I noticed a large male black bear standing on its rear feet with its front feet propped up on a log that was leaning against the log that I was leaning against. I'm sure he was hoping to find a nest full of turkey eggs and, if everything went well, to catch the turkey, too. Now he was staring at me with a very inquisitive look in his eye as he struggled to recalibrate his expectations.

I once heard a radio interview with a neuroscientist who studies mental processes during extremely stressful moments. He described how people in such situations will recall having dozens of distinct thoughts in the seconds that it takes for, say, a person that has fallen from a roof to hit the ground. His belief, he explained, is that we aren't actually having those thoughts when we think we are; rather, through a trick of memory, we just *think* we had them whenever we try to recall the moment. Regardless of what that guy says, I know that I had the following thoughts over the course of the next second or so: I thought about how weird it was that this bear and I both happened to be hunting turkeys in the same place at the same time; and I thought about how weird it was that I was trying to deceive a turkey in order to kill it and eat it, and how my efforts to do so had in turn deceived another creature that would have liked to have killed and eaten that turkey as well; and I wondered what effect my turkey gun, a twelve-gauge shotgun loaded with copper-coated #5 pellets, would have on a black bear at close range; and I imagined myself making a case for self-defense when I was investigated by a game warden for killing a black bear without the proper permit; and I imagined what it would be like to get mauled by a black bear; and, if I did get mauled, I imagined that it would be a very minor mauling as the bear would quickly realize that I wasn't what he was after; and then I thought about how black bears hardly ever mess with people; and then I imagined myself telling this story for a very long time, regardless of the actual outcome.

The bear interrupted this whirlwind litany of thoughts with a woof, like the first noise a dog might make when someone knocks at the door. He then ran off through the timber at the casual pace of a jogging human. The sound of the bear's running died away, and the forest returned to its usual crisp and breezy stillness. I leaned back to wait for my pulse to slow, as it was racing at a speed that I figured to be unhealthy. I sat for maybe five minutes, just breathing and thinking. I had that grateful and relieved feeling that you get when you first realize that you're recovering from the flu. Then I heard a turkey gobble, so far away and faint that the sound seemed more like a feeling than an actual noise. I got up to look for it, happy to be alive and walking in this wonderful and ancient world where bears sigh and turkeys gobble.

The second moment that helps answer the question of why I hunt occurred well over two thousand miles to the north of where I was hunting turkeys. I was camped on the North Slope of Alaska's Brooks Range, about seventy-five miles south of the Arctic Ocean's Beaufort Sea. I'd been there for a week, waiting for the arrival of caribou. I hadn't intended to stay so long, and I was running low on food. This was worrying me just as the sound of food came by. I was lying in my sleeping bag during the first moments of morning light, and the noise I heard was a rush of wings so close to my tent that the nylon quivered. It was followed by the strange cackling of ptarmigan, a grouse-like bird that is bigger than a quail but smaller than a pheasant. My brother Danny has heard their call described as *go-back, go-back, go-back,* but it reminds me more of Curly's signature laugh from the Three Stooges—a sort of *nyack-nyack-nyack.*

My boots were frozen, but I pulled them on as best as I could and stepped out to a gravel bar that was crusted in frost. I dragged a rubberized duffel bag out from under my flipped-over canoe, grabbed a twenty-gauge shotgun in one hand and a handful of shells in the other, and trotted off in the direction that the birds had gone. I crossed the ice of a small pond, formed where a braid of the river had become isolated from the main channel. It was almost frozen to the bottom, and I could see a small school of sticklebacks biding their time inside a doomed world. The pond ended at a steeply eroded cut bank. I pulled myself up the ledge and then rose to my feet. I was now standing on the soft, moss-padded ground of the tundra. The birds had already molted to their white winter plumage, though there was no snow yet. This was bad for them but good for me, as I could see them running along the ground as plainly as softballs rolling across a field.

I followed along. Soon I had them herded against a frozen pond, with a strong wind blowing from me to them. Birds need resistance against their wings in order to fly. During high winds they have to jump into the wind to lift off. So these birds were in a bad position— either jump into the wind and come right toward me, or expose themselves by running across the open ice. They were seemingly paralyzed by indecisiveness, and chose to do neither. According to some contemporary notions of sportsmanship, I should have flushed the birds into the air in order to give them more of a chance to escape before I started shooting. But I was hungry and in no mood to play with my chances, so I aligned the barrel with a few of their heads and pulled the trigger.

When I was done plucking the birds, the blood and the scattering of white feathers gave my campsite the appearance of a pillow fight gone horribly wrong. I poked a small incision into the belly of each bird, just below the point of its breastbone, and then wriggled two fingers into the incision and pulled out the wads of tangled-up organs. The gizzards, hearts, and livers went into the titanium coffee cup of my mess kit. I walked the birds to the river, reached out past the thin skein of ice along the edge, and dipped the birds into the current. A frill of pinkish water ran downstream. Using the index and middle finger of my right hand, I reached into the birds' chest cavities and scraped the lungs away from the insides of their backs. The purplish chunks of pulverized tissue vanished downstream.

I'd dragged my canoe nine miles upriver to this place, convinced that I'd find mixed groups of bulls and cows migrating through on their way toward the breeding and wintering grounds in and beyond the mountains to the south. But so far all I'd seen was a group of cows and calves headed the opposite way, toward the north. They didn't do me any good, regardless of which way they were headed, because all I could legally kill were bulls. I was allowed two of them, plenty of meat to get me through a year without having to buy any from a store. I'd kicked around the idea of moving another five or six miles upstream into fresh territory, but that seemed like a bad idea because entire stretches of the river were frozen solid up there. I'd just have to hold tight and trust my luck.

I hadn't taken a good look around that morning, so I set the meat from the birds on the flipped-over canoe and walked up to the top of the small rise behind my camp. With my binoculars, I checked for any caribou that might be drifting through. There were none. I couldn't see much at all to the north because the slope of the valley rose up sharply behind me, but I could see a good ways in every other direction. Stretching to the east and west was the braided and meandering valley of the river I was camped in, with its many small tributaries and oxbow lakes and gravel bars coated in felt-leaf willow and soapberry and locoweed. To the south, about a mile and a half away, a long ridgeline paralleled the valley. There was very strong atmospheric refraction in that direction; the seam between the land and the air shimmered and danced crazily, like an exaggerated version of heat waves coming off a highway in the desert. The day before, when two red foxes were screwing around up there, they looked like they had wire for legs. Four musk oxen came through a couple hours later; with the refraction and their long hair, they looked like ragged brown tents flapping in the breeze.

The Canadian-born explorer Vilhjalmur Stefansson, who passed through this same country just about a hundred years before me, talked a lot about the trickiness of Arctic light. He once mistook an up-close ground squirrel for a faraway grizzly. He tells of another hunter who mistook a three- or four-ounce lemming for a musk ox weighing several hundred pounds. He also mentions a man who steered his boat toward a "dark mountain with glacier-filled valleys on either side." The mountain then dove underwater as the man approached. It was actually a walrus's head, and the glaciers were its tusks.*

I walked back down the hill and stoked my fire using the root wads of willow trees that erode out of the riverbanks and collect at the heads of gravel bars in body-sized jumbles that look like storm-ravaged bird's nests. After dipping enough water in the cup to cover the organs, I set it on the coals to boil. Next I split two of the ptarmigan down the spine, filleted away the translucent plates of breastbone, and flattened the halves out with my palm. I melted a scoop of bacon grease in a pan and added the four halves of the birds. When everything was boiled and fried, I walked back up to the rise.

As my toes got numb in the cold air, I found myself longing for the warmer weather of August. But I reminded myself that warmer weather comes at a cost in the Arctic. The mosquitoes, blackflies, and warble flies can turn caribou hunting into a game of physical endurance. One time I took off my gloves to gut and skin a caribou and my fingers got so bitten and swollen that I could hardly close my hand around the knife. You hear accounts of insects killing caribou calves. They like to bite the places with short hair, like the lower legs, the areas around the eye, and the bellies. One time, south of here, my buddy Matt Moisan killed a bull that had an eye so densely surrounded with blackflies that I was reminded of those aerial photos taken from a blimp that show the rows of spectators around the empty space of a football field.

One August day a few years back, my friend Dan Bogan and I

*Funny thing about Stefansson: He once chopped the tongue from the desiccated corpse of a bowhead whale that he found washed up on the shore. He subsisted for days on the meat, often boiling it two or three times in an effort to remove the impregnated sea salts. Later, he learned from Eskimo hunters that the whale had been there for four years.

spent a whole day up on a hill that was shaped like a woman's chest. We were hiding in the cleavage, out of sight. It had been overcast and very windy, and we hadn't seen a single caribou. Then the wind died down and the sun came out, and so many blackflies settled on my back that it looked like my clothes had grown a layer of mold. A few minutes went by and a group of six caribou appeared over the crest of a distant ridge, working their way uphill in search of a breeze strong enough to put the bugs down. Two more groups appeared farther out. Suddenly another caribou appeared out of nowhere along the shore of a lake just a mile away. It was running full tilt, quartering away from us, and I followed it with my binoculars until I could see a rack of antlers towering over its head. "That's a bull," I said to Bogan. The bull was headed for a pair of lakes separated by a narrow isthmus, and it seemed like he'd be funneled along it. We raced over there, using a hill as cover, and by nightfall we were back at camp eating slices of fried caribou heart.

But now it was October instead of August, and instead of being plagued by flies I was plagued by a sense of futility. I had a brief moment of excitement when three caribou popped over the ridge to the north, headed roughly in my direction. But it only took a second or two for me to realize they were all cows. I watched as they followed the exact same northbound route as the small band that had passed through a few days earlier. There was nothing to signify a trail or a path, and I wondered what was guiding them. I walked eastward a quarter of a mile to look into their tracks. I wished that I could pull some kind of shaman's trick to understand where they were going and whether bulls were following them. But instead, the only thing the tracks revealed to me was my own sense of wonder.

I started back toward the rise as a strange fog blew in from the coast. It came so thick and solid that it looked like it could scrape up my tent and carry it away, but then it began to break up into gauzy wisps that drifted over the land like bedsheets caught in the wind. Just as one of these sheets passed me by, I looked to the right and watched as a herd of caribou came over the ridgeline and spilled toward me like a landslide of muscle draped in colors of brown and white and gray. Floating above this body was a tangled forest of antler. They were all bulls.

They reached the river within seconds. If they'd kept coming in that same direction, they would have crossed the river and passed right next to me. But instead they turned sharply to the right and ran upstream. To pursue them, I would have to drop off the rise and lose sight of the herd. Something told me not to do this, to hold tight and watch where they went. But something stronger said to go.

I grabbed my rifle and pack and headed off as fast as possible, trying to parallel their route upstream. I ran until my lungs ached, without catching any glimpse of the animals ahead of me. I covered about a mile or so of tundra before I got to another piece of high ground. From up there, I still could not see the bulls on the opposite side of the river. They had vanished, either by continuing upstream around a bend in the river or else by dropping down into the hopelessly thick tangle of willows that carpeted the valley floor. My initial impulse was to keep moving upstream, but then I noticed something about the contours of the land. Across the river, a slight gully led from the hills into the valley floor. It seemed to provide a good avenue of travel down from the high bank. A matching gully, just a little offset, cut down through the bank on my side. Between the gullies, the valley floor was not as thickly packed with willow as the rest of it was. It seemed like a feature that the caribou might utilize.

I entered the gully and followed it down into the river valley. It terminated at a dry stream channel that was as wide as a driveway. I could see a hundred yards in each direction, upstream and downstream, but only about thirty yards in the direction that I hoped the caribou would come from. I hid myself behind a clump of willows, laid out my backpack, and positioned the barrel of my rifle across the pack for support.

Minutes passed and nothing happened. Then more minutes passed and still nothing happened. I got a sinking feeling in my gut. The river valley was only so wide, and the caribou had been moving fast. They should have come through already. I thought about racing upriver as a last-ditch effort, but I recognized now that it was too late for that. If they'd run that way, they were long gone by now. After another minute I stood up to try to get a look across the tops of the willows. And then occurred the simple moment that I've been leading up to, the sort of moment that helps me to explain why I hunt: I was hungry in the wilderness and here came a few tons' worth of caribou, fifty yards out and closing fast. In a moment like that, there is no time for emotional dawdling. It is a time for unerring judgment. It is a time for speed, both mental and physical. It is a time for action and precision and discipline. It is a time to do what millions of years' worth of evolution built us to do. And in the act of doing it, you experience the unconfused purity of being a human predator, stripped of everything that is nonessential. In that moment of impending violence and death, you are gifted a beautiful glimpse of life.

When I consider all the astonishing and inspiring things that happen to hunters, it puzzles me that so many people have turned away from the lifestyle. At this moment, in a per capita sense, there are fewer hunters on earth than at any other time in human history. Only about 5 percent of Americans hunt, down from about 7 percent a decade ago. In California, Massachusetts, and New Jersey, only about 1 percent of the population hunts. Oddly, our country has more golfers than hunters. I wonder how this could have happened. In a way, I see golf as a revolt against hunting. As a nation, we have swapped the smelly and unpredictable pungency of the woods in exchange for the sanitized safety of manicured grass. While we once wondered about the migrations of wild animals across the landscape, we now wonder whether the putting greens will be slow or fast. While we once pushed deep into the wilderness in search of herds that have been untouched by other men, we now ask politely if we can play through. While we once feasted on venison liver seared over an open fire and washed back with creek water, we now buy beer from a cooler fixed to the back of a motorized cart parked on a gravel pathway.

Of course, we still have a good number of fishermen, which is heartening to me. I've always tended to think of fishing as a variation on hunting. I mean this in a historical way, in that primitive human beings learned to fish as an offshoot of hunting and they often pursued fish with the same types of weapons that they used in the pursuit of land-based creatures; and I also mean this in a philosophical way, in that many modern people are motivated to fish by the same factors that motivate them to hunt, things such as adventure, communion with nature, physical activity, a love of process and acquired skill, and a desire for an intimate connection to one's food. What's more, hunting and fishing sometimes just *feel* the same way. Take halibut fishing. To catch a halibut, one usually ventures into dangerous waters in a wilderness setting. The fish are big, sometimes as big as a deer. When you get one to the boat, it can be necessary to shoot it with a rifle or shotgun in order to kill it. If you don't do this, the fish can break your arm. Once it's dead, removing the meat from a big halibut has a lot more to do with butchering than it does with filleting. You can get enough meat from one halibut to feed yourself and your friends dinner for weeks. Considering all this, you can see why I might think of halibut fishing as a form of big-game hunting, except that the primary implement happens to be a hook rather than a bullet.

Perhaps more troubling than the overall decline of American hunters is the overall increase in Americans who are uneasy with hunting. Today, about one-fifth of all Americans are outright opposed to the practice. A casual summation of the various anti-hunting stances would be that times have changed and hunters no longer hunt for reasons of food, cultural continuity, and a love for the outdoors; instead, hunters just want to kill animals in order to prove their manliness and get their jollies.

The argument about how we don't rely on the meat puzzles me, because it makes me wonder what exactly my family has been eating for dinner every night. The argument about proving our manliness has some merit, and I will touch on that later on. The jollies argument is much less interesting, but I would like to quickly address a practical issue that it brings up: If hunters really did get their jollies by killing animals, why would we go through the hassle of trying to find wild and unpredictable game animals under sometimes exceedingly difficult environmental circumstances when we could just volunteer at the Humane Society and kill a few dozen dogs and cats in an afternoon, or get a job at an Iowa slaughterhouse and kill a couple hundred cattle a day in air-conditioned comfort?

If you read hunting magazines or look at opinion polls, you might be tempted to think that the cultural debate about hunting is something new, that contemporary human society is just now making a rapid, fundamental, and inexorable shift that threatens to turn hunters into anachronistic outlaws. The truth is that this debate has occurred over much of human history. The Bible itself includes a nod to the tension between hunters and nonhunters. When Isaac's wife, Rebekah, gives birth to twin boys, the first to emerge is Esau, a baby covered in thick fur, "like an hairy garment." Clinging to his heel is his brother Jacob. "And the boys grew: and Esau was a cunning hunter, a man of the field; and Jacob was a plain man, dwelling in tents."

These boys get on each other's nerves right away. Esau the Hunter is loved by his father, Isaac, "who did eat of his venison," whereas Jacob, the smooth-skinned and stay-at-home farmer, is more of a mama's boy. One day, Esau is out hunting with his bow. As any bow hunter knows, this can be a dicey proposition. And, sure enough, Esau comes wandering home so hungry that he's about to faint. (I've been there.) He comes across Jacob and begs his twin brother for some lentils. Jacob refuses to give him any unless Esau agrees to surrender to him his rights as the firstborn son. It's unclear whether Esau doesn't take the deal seriously or doesn't care that much about his birthright or really is just that hungry, but in any case he makes the trade and eats the lentils.

Years go by. Eventually, the father of the two brothers grows old and blind, and one day he calls his eldest son to his side and makes a request. He tells Esau to gather his weapons, "thy quiver and thy bow," and "go out to the field, and take me some venison." If Esau does this, Isaac promises that he'll give him his blessing before he dies. So Esau gathers up his gear and heads out to hunt.

What happens next is further testament to the difficulty of bow hunting: Esau is gone so long that his mother and brother have time to execute an elaborate betrayal. Rebekah sends Jacob out to kill one of his domestic sheep. She tells him to dress himself in the sheep's fleece, and to prepare the animal's meat in the style of venison. Jacob does this, and then approaches his blind father. Isaac feels the sheep's wool on Jacob's back and mistakes it for the hair of his firstborn son. He also mistakes the sheep's meat for his beloved venison. Thus deceived, Isaac bestows his blessing upon the wrong son. *

---

*Don't be alarmed if this is confusing. Biblical scholars have long struggled with the apparent redundancy presented by Jacob both buying his brother's birthright and tricking him out of it. There are a few "official" theories about why this happened, and I will supplement these with one or two of my own: 1) With the lentils, Jacob was actually buying from Esau the right to later trick him out of his birthright (which seems

Esau's hunting story distresses me even more than the popularity of a game like golf. It suggests that the passage of hunting has been predicted from ancient times. That Esau the hunter emerged out of the womb ahead of Jacob the farmer, and that the farmer eventually won out over the hunter, is certainly consistent with a secular understanding of human history. While many of the details are hazy and incomplete and often disputed, it's generally agreed that anatomically and behaviorally modern humans emerged on the scene in Africa less than a hundred thousand years ago. (In other words, if you took an infant from that period and put him into a time machine set for today, he wouldn't look terribly out of place and he'd be able to learn how to fly a plane and download applications on his phone.) We now know these people as the "ancestral human population." There may have been as few as five thousand of them, and they had all the hallmarks of humanity: They had complex language; they lived in shelters of their own making; they were organized into family units and clans; they played music; they made art; they probably cut and styled their hair; they developed trade networks; they wore fitted clothing; and they were skilled hunters capable of taking down dangerous big-game animals with intricate hunting weapons made from bone, ivory, and antler.

It's astounding how quickly the ancestors of these hunters spread around the world. They left Africa maybe 50,000 or 60,000 years ago.* They were in Australia by 45,000 years ago. They were in France and

---

strange); 2) there's a missing passage in the Bible, in which Esau reveals to Jacob that he had merely psyched him out with the lentil deal and hadn't actually meant it, which means that Jacob had to go steal the birthright all over again (which also seems strange); 3) Jacob was thorough in his acquisitions and didn't feel as though something was really his until he had both purchased it and swindled for it (also strange); 4) we do not know enough for the story to make total sense, and these sorts of inquiries are pointless.

*These numbers are hotly debated, and may never be settled with any degree of satisfaction.

Germany 36,000 years ago, where they hunted wild horses by driving them off cliffs. By 20,000 years ago they were way up in Siberia, using spears to kill such animals as yaks, mammoths, short-faced bears, and woolly rhinoceros. They crossed the Bering Strait into Alaska maybe around 14–15,000 years ago, and were camped all the way down in South America just a thousand or so years later. Thirteen thousand years ago, hunters left behind a semipermanent encampment in southern Chile that now shows evidence of shellfish carapaces, fish bones, eggshells, llama bones, broken mastodon ribs, scraps of butchered meat, tools made of stone and ivory, a cache of salt, wooden timbers, and tent stakes wrapped in mastodon rawhide.

At the time that camp was occupied, pretty much all habitable environments outside of a few isolated island chains in the remotest oceanic corners had been colonized by hunter-gatherers. Several more millennia would pass before agriculture made its appearance in the vicinity of Iraq about 10,000 years ago. It would be independently invented in the New World maybe 5,000 years later. On the most basic level, agriculture leads to more food; more food leads to more people; more people leads to professional specialization; professional specialization leads to invention; invention leads to the development of greater weapons; the development of greater weapons leads to conquest. What this meant, over the centuries, is that agricultural people basically kicked the shit out of hunters. They did it in physical ways, like the way Mayan agrarians killed and enslaved hunter-gatherers on the periphery of their empire; they did it in cultural ways, like how mainland Europeans introduced the Paleolithic hunters of the British Isles to agriculture without physically displacing them; and they did it in ways that were both physically *and* culturally overwhelming, like the way that Europeans managed to effectively swallow and digest the continents of Africa, Australia, North America, and South America.

At the beginning of European contact in what is now the United

States, the most powerful cultures—the Iroquois Confederacy, the Mississippian tribes—had risen to dominance on the shoulders of agriculture. That these groups were the first to fall to European conquest is an unusual twist on the typical story of agriculture's relentless destruction of hunters around the world. Agricultural tribes in the Americas were confined to stationary locations and were packed closely together. This made them easy to locate and wage war against. More important, it opened them up to the rapid transmission of infectious diseases inadvertently introduced by Europeans. The more nomadic peoples who ranged across the land as loosely structured bands of hunters were harder to locate and subjugate. They held out for quite a bit longer. In the United States, the last free-roaming tribes of indigenous hunters weren't rounded up or killed off or driven away until about the year 1876. Fourteen years later, the U.S. Census Bureau declared that the American frontier had officially closed. Farmers had filled the place up.

All of the above is a way of saying that we've probably entered a period that will one day be regarded as the autumn of hunting. However, you should not consider this book to be an act of submission. It is not a tearful farewell. Rather, I think of hunting—and of writing about it—as a form of resistance. It's an insurgency, an act of guerrilla warfare against the inevitable advance of time.

As inspiration, I think of a piece of fossilized bone that a man found a few years ago near Vero Beach, Florida. Carved into the bone, which measures about fifteen inches by four inches, is an unmistakable image of a mastodon or mammoth: tail, legs, trunk, tusks, ears. Whoever carved that bone had certainly laid eyes on the subject of his work, so he must have lived during the very short window of time when man's presence in Florida overlapped with the presence of mastodons and mammoths—about thirteen thousand years ago. A short while after he carved it, perhaps just a matter of years or centuries, the animals were extinct. Perhaps the man knew that this was coming when he carved the bone; perhaps that's *why* he carved the bone. His clan of mammoth hunters would need to find a new way to live. Or maybe, for all he knew, life would end altogether. And so he sat down and etched his own version of a hunting story into the bone. Then thousands and thousands of years went by. And along comes a guy who picks up the bone without noticing the carving. He puts the bone in a box under his sink. Still more years go by. And then he picks up the bone and cleans it off and gives it a look.

The bone speaks to him: *I am a hunter. This is my story.*

CHAPTER TWO

Stirring the Limbs

★

HUNTERS SELDOM ASK each other how they got into hunting. If I had to guess, I'd say this is because they already know the answer. The vast majority of hunters throughout the great span of human history have hunted because their fathers did. Of course, one could argue that many hunters in indigenous cultures had little choice in the matter— they either had to learn to hunt or they would starve to death. That's a perfectly valid point, as the hunting lifestyle wasn't just one of several options available to, say, a member of the Koyukon tribe who was born a few hundred years ago along Alaska's Koyukuk River. But the lack of options hardly negates the importance of fathers to the tradition of hunting. Not only did Koyukon boys hunt because their fathers hunted, Koyukon boys *survived* because their fathers hunted.

While there are some notable exceptions to the rule of patrilineal descent among modern-day hunters (my dad included, as you'll see), I'm definitely not one of them. Plain and simple, I am a hunter because he was. However, I hardly do things just because my dad did them. If anything, I'd say the opposite is true. For instance, he used to make me pull old rusty nails out of rotting boards with a crowbar and then straighten them for reuse with a ball-peen hammer and an anvil. If I need a nail today, I'll just go out and buy a box of them. But there was something about my father's relationship to hunting that appealed to me in a very direct and immediate way. I was too young then to articulate it, but I see now that it had to do with freedom, strength, and self-sufficiency. My dad was tough and he knew how to take care of himself, no matter what happened, and I was his student. I could reel in bluegills by the age of three, and I was hunting small game by the age of seven. It was early enough that I have no recollection of the first fish that I caught or the first squirrels and rabbits that I ever harvested. Instead, when I try to remember back to some early experience in hunting, my first memory is of a day when my two brothers and I were already out from under the protection of our dad.

I know that it was September 15, because it was the opening day of Michigan's annual squirrel hunting season. And I know it was 1984, because my dad gave me my first .22 when I turned ten. I was carrying it as I walked through the woods with my two older brothers, Matt and Danny. We were headed toward a patch of forest that we called the Camp Woods, because it was owned by an old summer camp that was mostly shut down by then. This area, on the western side of the state, had once been a thriving region for summer camps and tourist cottages before it became a place where people chose to live full-time. In fact, the Remington I was carrying once belonged to another such camp as part of their marksmanship program. Before that camp closed, my brothers and I used to sneak in there and sift the sand from the rifle range's backdrop through wire mesh screens in order to get the bullet lead. We'd melt it down with propane torches and then pour it into molds for making fishing sinkers.

Ahead we could see Mueller Road, the dirt lane that separated the Camp Woods from the patch of woods that sat right across the road from our own house. We weren't supposed to fire our guns until we crossed that road, because our dad didn't want us shooting so close to

*My brothers Danny (left) and Matt (right) and me on the shore of
Middle Lake in the mid-1980s. Before you laugh at Matt's shorts,
please bear in mind that my mother made them.*

home. Sometimes we'd find a squirrel in the woods by the house and
then follow it until it crossed Mueller Road and became fair game.
The oaks on either side of that road grew out toward each other like
they were trying to form an archway. I was always amazed by the way
a squirrel would risk a six-foot leap across the gap rather than just
come down to the ground and walk across. My dad liked to tell me
that in the days of Daniel Boone a squirrel could travel all the way
from the Atlantic coast to the Mississippi River without ever touching
the ground—all it had to do was jump from tree to tree. I'm sure he
meant this as a way of highlighting the differences between mine and
Boone's worlds, but I simply took it as a testament to the fact that a
squirrel was a good jumper. In fact, I would have been willing to bet
that a squirrel could whip a monkey in a treetop race, even though I
had absolutely no experience with monkeys except for a stuffed one
that hung in the entryway of my great-uncle Gunner's house. He said

the monkey bit off two of his fingers when he was a kid and the zoo gave him the stuffed carcass as a form of condolence. Uncle Gunner was, in fact, missing a few fingers on his right hand, but my mom later explained that he'd actually lost them to his lawn mower.

We crossed Mueller Road cautiously and quietly, to make sure no one saw us. We weren't hiding for any particular reason, but we considered hunting to be a secretive activity. Daniel Boone would walk across downed trees rather than risk leaving a track on the ground that someone might find. Besides, I enjoyed sneaking across Mueller Road with my rifle. It reminded me of the cover of one of my favorite books, *The Light in the Forest.* It's the fictional story of a white boy on the American frontier in the 1700s. When the story begins, he'd been kidnapped by Indians eleven years earlier. The Indians adopted him and raised him as their own, and he grew up with hardly a memory of being a white person. Eventually, though, the military comes to recover him as part of a peace deal. The book goes on to tell the awful story of what happens to this boy when he's returned to the whites, and then it tells the awful story of what happens when he gets away from the whites and rejoins the Indians.

On the cover of this book is a painting of two bare-chested boys, one Indian and one ghostly white, both with Mohawk haircuts and buckskin leggings. The white boy is carrying a rifle, the Indian, a bow. The boys are presented in such a way that the viewer can just catch a glimpse of them as they move through a gap in the forest. And in the moment that I stepped from the dark of the woods and into the light of Mueller Road, it was easy for me to imagine myself as the boy from the cover of that book, traveling through the forest with an Indian. I kept such fantasies to myself, mostly out of embarrassment. But I now see that you can't overemphasize the role of wild Indians in the imaginations of all young boys who love to be in the woods. We grow up in one of two ways: either wanting to be a wild Indian or wanting to be

a white man who hunted among wild Indians. It's the difference between boys who want to wear feathers in their hair and boys who
want to wear coonskin caps. Those who want to be Indians do not
generally turn into hunters, but those who want to be whites among
Indians do. I'm not sure why this is true, but I'm guessing it might
have something to do with attainability. Maybe boys who want to be
Indians get overwhelmed by the futility of their quest; they'll never
change their skin. But boys like me, who grow up wanting to hunt
with Indians, only have to lose a portion of their fantasy to achieve it.

It doesn't hurt that the celebrated heroes of American history include dozens and dozens of white hunters who made their lives among
Indians. As a kid I had memorized their names and stories, learned
their faces from sketches and photos. There were the men of America's first frontier, like Boone and Simon Kenton, who ranged across
the Appalachian Mountains. And then there were the mountain men
of the Rockies, like Jim Bridger and Jed Smith. I knew that Boone
once killed more than a hundred black bears in a fall and smoked all
the meat and sold it as "bear bacon"; I knew that he passed through
the Cumberland Gap on a hunting trip to the wilderness of Kentucky,
and later opened a trail through there so his family could follow; I
knew that he didn't try to see Indians hiding in the bushes, but instead looked for the unnaturally straight barrels of their rifles; and I
knew that he was captured and adopted by the Shawnee Indians, and
that he enjoyed hunting with his captors so much that his own people
put him on trial for treason when he finally escaped. I saw no reason
that I shouldn't have a life of adventure like that, and I knew that
hunting was my way to do it.

The understory of the Camp Woods was mostly sassafras and
honeysuckle, with a thigh-high layer of ferns around their bases. My
brothers and I liked to dig out the sassafras roots to boil them into a
tea that smelled and tasted like root beer. Overhead, the canopy was

almost a solid mat of oak leaves punctured here and there by large white pines that jutted out like disheveled church steeples above the skyline of an old town. We considered these white pines to be an annoyance, especially once the hardwoods lost their leaves in the late fall. At that time of year squirrels got super-wary, probably because the lack of leaves exposed them to predators like hawks and owls. And since they were on heightened alert, a human intruder into their area sent them booking through the treetops toward the crown of the nearest white pine. Once a squirrel got into a white pine, he vanished into the upper limbs so thoroughly that it was pointless to bother looking for him.

But at this time of year, mid-September, the white pines weren't nearly as much of an issue. The leaves seemed to give the squirrels a sense of security and they were less likely to take off if they saw you. Also, the leaves were helpful because they greatly amplified the noises a squirrel made as he picked acorns in the canopy. This is what was going on in front of us now. Leaves were shaking overhead, and there was the pitter-patter of shucked acorn husks falling to the ground. At first it seemed as if a whole gang of squirrels were up there, but as we deciphered the noises it sounded more like there were maybe just two or three in one particular oak. The rest of the noise was birds. Without needing to discuss the plan, we separated and began sneaking in toward the trees.

Matt and Danny were carrying shotguns, which meant they could knock a squirrel out of a tree even it was running from limb to limb. They'd gotten them for Christmas when they reached Michigan's legal hunting age of twelve. Matt was now thirteen; he'd already killed two deer with his bow. I had yet to get my shotgun. According to the law, I wasn't even allowed to hunt squirrels with a BB gun at my age. But my parents were reluctant to establish and enforce different sets of rules among us. They generally figured that if one of us could do something, we all could. The one difference was that, for now, I had to do it with a .22.

Suddenly I heard a slight whoosh overhead. I froze dead still and moved my eyes in the direction of the sound without moving my head too much. Sure enough, I could see a dark blob of solid material among the leaves toward the end of the limb. I could tell by the squirrel's size and shape that it was a fox squirrel. While we had greater respect for gray squirrels, which we considered to be warier and woodsier because we tended to find them in the darker forests and ravine bottoms, we admired fox squirrels for their size. We'd gotten a few large males that were so big they had back hams almost like a rabbit's.

This one was about a hundred feet up in the tree. I waited until he was busy shucking another acorn before I dared to raise my rifle. When I did, I rested the barrel against a small oak tree. With a shotgun I could have shot the squirrel as it bobbed around behind the curtain of fluttering leaves. But my dad was an advocate of hitting squirrels in the head with a .22, and so I had to wait for a clear shot. One time, a few years later, we were hunting with our dad and we killed a whole bunch of squirrels* with our shotguns while our dad killed only two with a .22. He said that his two were better than all of ours put together, because he didn't mess up any meat and there was no worry of busting your tooth on a shotgun pellet while you ate. But what he didn't understand was that he hunted squirrels because he liked to eat them; we, on the other hand, hunted squirrels because we liked to hunt them. Busting teeth wasn't something we were particularly concerned about.

---

*In Michigan, the daily bag limit for squirrels is five. There's a possession limit of ten, which means you're not supposed to have more than that in your freezer at any one time. Other states, such as Montana, do not recognize squirrels as a game animal and there is no limit. The daily bag limit in New York state is six. In California, four.

Legend has it that Daniel Boone killed squirrels by doing something called "barking" them. The rifles that the frontiersmen used to kill deer and bear and Indians were too big for squirrels—they ruined too much meat. So Boone would aim for a patch of tree bark next to the squirrel. The shock from the bullet hitting the wood was so strong that it killed the squirrel and sent it flying.* As much as I would have loved to do that, there was no way a .22 was up to the task.

I was still waiting for my clean shot when the squirrel suddenly bolted toward the base of the tree. He'd seen me. When he got there, he headed outward again along an opposing branch. When he hit the tip of that limb, he launched himself into the air and landed in another tree with a whoosh of leaves. He ran toward the trunk of that tree and vanished.

Matt and Danny came walking over and stared into the tree with me. There was a white pine a couple of trees away, and Danny went toward it in case the squirrel tried to head that way. The first thing Matt and I did was start looking for nests and holes, which are almost as bad as white pines when it comes to hiding squirrels. A squirrel nest looks like a bird's nest except it tends to be more ball-shaped than disk-shaped. Some of them are as big as an eagle's nest. It's frustrating when a squirrel runs into his nest because you know right where he is and you know that he's protected only by a buffer of leaves. When we hunted with BB guns, we'd fire right into the nests. A BB gun is almost never instantly fatal to a squirrel, so even if you hit the animal he'd still have enough life in him to flop free of the nest before

*The famed naturalist and painter John James Audubon claimed to have joined Boone in the task of barking squirrels along the Kentucky River in 1810. Boone's shot sent "the squirrel whirling through the air, as if it had been blown up by the explosion of a powder magazine." Apparently, this strategy worked very well for Boone. "Before many hours had elapsed," claims Audubon, "we had procured as many squirrels as we wished." Historians have since questioned the veracity of this claim, as it seems that Boone was not in the state of Kentucky in 1810. He was in Missouri.

he dropped. But with a .22 or shotgun you could feasibly kill him right in the nest and he'd never come out. This wasn't a big worry if it was the kind of nest you could climb up to. But usually squirrels are smart enough to build their nests in places that are inaccessible to terrestrial predators.

It was obvious that there weren't any nests around, though we did find a place where a limb had broken away from the trunk. There was a cavity in the center of the remaining stub, and there was a white ring around it from squirrels that had been chewing on it to expand the hole. Sure enough, that was probably where the squirrel had gone. I stared up at the hole for a few moments, thinking that I'd get lucky and he'd poke his head out for a look. But Matt and Danny knew that this was pointless. They'd already started drifting away through the woods. I followed after them, unsure where we'd ultimately end up.

I got a tremendous sense of freedom from being in the woods like this, from wandering with no constraints. The hunting woods were a place where my brothers and I were our own men. We didn't get as much of that as we wanted—I don't imagine any boys do, really—because our dad liked to keep us busy with chores. He drew them up in lists of twenty-eight, because that's how many lines were on his legal pads and apparently he didn't want to waste any space. Some of the chores on these lists were necessary and easily accomplished, such as putting in the garden and cleaning the garage, but others were knuckle-bustingly hard and mind-numbingly boring. One summer, for instance, he made us move an old pile of rotten leaves and then replace it with an old pile of red bricks from a demolished building. We then spent the summer knocking all the old mortar off the bricks with hammers and cold chisels so that they could be used to build a circular fire pit.

This past summer had been particularly grueling, because he'd come across a trailer load of used railroad ties from a crew that was ripping out a length of track. He'd concocted a plan for a tiered system of walkways in an area of the yard that no one ever had any business walking in except if they were going over there to do chores. Because the ties were decayed on the ends, and the hollow portions had accumulated an abundance of dirt and gravel that would destroy the bar and chain on our chain saw, we had to cut the ties to length using an antique two-man crosscut logging saw that had been hanging as a decoration on the cedar siding of our home. Then, using two sets of old-fashioned ice tongs that had been hanging next to the crosscut saw, we had to drag the ties to the job site and bed them in place. Every evening, after we got a few of the ties anchored in place with lengths of steel rebar, the old man would come out with a four-foot bubble level to check our work. Any ties that were off-level had to come back out and get reset. This went on for three months, nonstop.*

I mention these chores in order to show what I was escaping, and I don't mean escaping in the sense that I headed into the woods to hide from my dad. By far, the fear of him coming to look for me was way worse than the fear of being around him. Rather, hunting in the woods provided me with an excuse of absence that my old man considered to be acceptable. He respected hunting, even encouraged it. At the time this baffled me, because I couldn't figure out why he'd surrender his workforce in order to let us chase squirrels. But now that I have my own son I understand his thinking a little better. He wanted his kids to be disciplined, tough, resourceful, and humble—he wanted

*I finally assumed the task of ripping those now completely rotten railroad ties out of the ground twenty years later. They'd become colonized by ground wasps, and I was stung so severely that I had to pay a visit to the emergency room in Muskegon. In all seriousness, not one single person ever took an honest walk along those walkways— fulfilling a prediction that I'd been punished for making two decades earlier.

us to be survivors. And he saw physical labor and hunting as equally viable paths toward that goal.

As the three of us continued westward, we ascended a slight ridge where the oaks were bigger than anywhere else in the Camp Woods. We leaned against the trees and listened, but no leaves rustled. The squirrels were there, no doubt, but they weren't giving themselves up. We walked down the other side of the ridge. At the base, we entered an area of smaller oaks where we seldom saw squirrels. We walked quickly through that area and didn't pause until we came to the edge of Staple Road. A squirrel that wanted to cross this road had to come down to the ground in order to do so. It was a two-lane blacktop, wide enough that the oaks on either side of the road couldn't reach out overhead far enough for a squirrel to be able to make the leap. We stood in the woods near the edge of Staple Road and watched and listened for a few moments. When we were sure no cars were coming, we trotted across the road into the trees.

Technically we'd been trespassing all along, since we didn't have

My father in a moment of levity. Here he wears a hat made from a raccoon that I killed. He's holding an orphaned pet raccoon that was given to me by a friend.

permission to be in the Camp Woods. But that hardly mattered to us, because we'd never gotten chased by anyone for being there and we considered it to be sort of like our own property. But the woods we were in now were absolutely off-limits; it was one of the few woods in the area that someone had actually bothered to mark with No Trespassing signs. The guy who owned it had some gutted-out appliances scattered around the entrance to his driveway, which was long and curved so you couldn't see the end of it from the road. None of us had ever gotten a really clean look at the place, but from here in the woods you could look through the trees and make out the shapes of vehicles and a shed and a house. Supposedly he would come after you if he caught you on his land. We'd seen where he took some earth-moving equipment one time and used it to pile up stumps to block an old motorbike trail that followed a natural gas pipeline across his property. That made him seem plenty serious.

Normally we'd move into woods and get out of sight of his home before making any noise, but right away we spooked a gray squirrel out of a small oak tree. "There's one," someone said. The squirrel leapt toward the trunk of a larger oak and hit with the sandpapery sound of claw on bark. He corkscrewed up the tree, covering about twelve feet of elevation in a single rotation of the trunk. We ran to surround the tree so that the squirrel would be in view of one of us at all times. The squirrel zipped past my side of the tree but didn't stop long enough for me to shoot. But Matt's shotgun boomed as the squirrel made his way past him. The blast was followed by a couple of seconds of silence and then the thud of the squirrel hitting the ground followed by the swishing of leaves as it flopped around. An eruption of dog barking came from the house, followed by what sounded like a slamming car door. Matt grabbed up his squirrel by the tail and the three of us ran.

It was thrilling to be scared like that, thrilling to have danger in the woods. It was just one more thing that bound me to my heroes, who kept death and danger as close to them as their rifles. They hunted the best land out there, and they paid for it. After he was mutilated by a grizzly, Jed Smith was killed by a Comanche who buried a tomahawk in his head. Jim Bridger lived through many skirmishes, and once spent a few years carrying two Indian arrowheads stuck in his back. Simon Kenton was tortured for days by Indians who punched a hole through his skull with a hammer, busted his collarbone and arm with an ax and a club, and then tried a couple of times to burn him at the stake. John Colter was forced to stand on the banks of a river while Indian warriors pelted him with the lungs and testicles of his slaughtered hunting partner.

Boone suffered as much as anyone. In 1773, his eldest son, James, was shot and tortured and mutilated by Indians near the Cumberland Gap; in 1780, Boone and his brother Ned were shucking hickory nuts along a trail in the Ohio Territory when Daniel took off after a bear that came wandering through. He gave chase and killed it, then returned to find Shawnee Indians celebrating over Ned's murdered body because they believed, mistakenly, that they'd killed the mighty Daniel Boone. Two years later, in 1782, Boone's son Israel was killed next to him by a shot through the neck fired by Indians at the Battle of Blue Licks. That my own hunting grounds might prove dangerous seemed only right.

We didn't stop running until we hit the old blocked-off trail that followed the gas pipeline. While we waited for any noises that might betray a pursuer, Matt laid his squirrel on the leaves. It was a male, with a scrotum the size of a big lima bean. Male squirrels have been known to castrate each other in fights, and we considered intact squirrels to be lucky. Most of the shotgun pellets had ended up in the head and neck. The old man might compliment us on that. Matt slipped the tip of his knife between the squirrel's rear legs and cut through its pelvic bone. Then he made a shallow cut up the squirrel's belly, just beneath the abdominal lining, all the way from the base of the tail to the ribs. He kept going and split the rib cage right where the two halves meet. Then he reached in and grabbed the heart with his fingertips and tugged out the entire package of guts. The inside of the squirrel was clean and glistening.

The rest we'd do at home: take a sharp knife and cut through the squirrel's hide all the way around its belly, right where a belt would sit if squirrels wore belts; then peel the bisected hide in both directions at once, the bottom half off like a pair of pants and the top half off like a shirt, until the hide was connected to the squirrel by nothing but the four feet, the head, and the tail; free it by severing the ankles, neck, and the base of the tail; then split the squirrel into five parts, the four legs and the back. Three or four squirrels cleaned like this would inspire my dad to heat up the deep fryer, or better yet, they'd inspire my mom to get out the Crock-Pot and cook the squirrels in a bath of cream of mushroom soup.

When the dogs quit barking and the woods went quiet, we crossed the pipeline and entered a marshy area where we'd jumped up grouse and woodcock in the past. But it had been a wet summer and water covered the ground in the brushy areas where the birds liked to hang out. Instead two wood ducks busted out of there so close that Matt and Danny said they could have had them both. But duck season was still over a month away. And while we'd shoot a squirrel out of season now and then, there was no way in hell that we'd ever kill a duck out of season. Our dad told us that many species of ducks had almost been wiped out by hunters in his own lifetime, and that he'd personally watched poachers in Arkansas shooting ducks off the water with large-bore shotguns that were mounted to the gunwale of a boat and fired all at once with the pull of a string. The sight had made him sick. The previous autumn, we were hauling leaves to the leaf pile in the woods when we stumbled across a bunch of plastic garbage bags that were full of wood ducks. There were forty in all, with nothing but the breast meat taken out. Forty ducks is way over the legal bag limit, even if the hunter happened to be hunting with four or five other guys. My old man conducted a little investigation and learned that the ducks belonged to a neighbor who had just moved into a nearby cottage. According to this man's son, he had once killed a dog with a baseball bat because it was chewing on the carcass of a deer that he had killed and hung from the rafters of his carport. Despite this, my old man went down to the beach and told the guy that he better watch out for trouble if he was going to be shooting that many ducks.

We separated around the pond, Danny following one shore and Matt and I going the other way. When we met back up we could see the occasional flash of a car going by on White Lake Drive. We moved ahead to the edge of the road and waited until there were no cars coming. We jogged across and dropped into a little bog with some blueberry bushes in it. We paralleled White Lake Drive in an easterly direction, staying just deep enough in the woods to pass behind the two houses along that road. A few years earlier, a single-engine airplane had crashed in these same woods. It was carrying a man in his fifties and a twelve-year-old boy who wasn't his son. My brothers and I showed up in time to watch them pull the bodies out. I remember a firefighter removing the boy's torso from the hole that the plane tore into the ground. The torso was missing its head and appendages, yet it still wore a T-shirt that you could tell was baby blue despite all the blood.

After walking a ways, we passed the intersection where Staple Road ended at White Lake Drive. We then sneaked back across into the Camp Woods. In about an hour it would be what our dad called "prime time," which was the last hour of the day, when the deer movements peaked. But a squirrel's schedule ran a little ahead of a deer's, so they'd probably start moving any minute now. We headed back up toward the ridge with the oaks, and this time the trees were alive with squirrels. We spread apart. I went off to the left and hit the top of the ridge beneath an oak where a squirrel had been shaking around. I couldn't see him now, but then I hadn't seen anything to indicate that he'd left. He was probably just holding tight.

I started walking circles around the tree to see if I could catch a glimpse of him, which hardly ever works if you're alone. That's because a squirrel will just walk around the tree ahead of you, keeping the trunk between you. A trick for this is to tie a string to a sapling on one side of the tree and stomp back to the opposite side. Holding the string in your hand, take a seat in a place where you have a good view of the tree but you're still a little bit hidden. Obviously the squirrel will know where you are and it will stay on the opposite side of the tree—the side where the string is tied to the sapling. Within a few minutes, though, the squirrel's memory will start to fade. He'll become increasingly unsure of what's going on. After a few more minutes, you give the string a sharp pull in order to shake the sapling. If you're lucky, the squirrel will think you've doubled back on him and will come zipping around to the side you're actually on.

I didn't try this, because I suspected the squirrel was up there lying on top of a limb, belly down, with his tail laid flat to the bark so it didn't give him away. We called this bellying a limb, and when a squirrel does it he's nearly impossible to see. I walked away from the tree to get a more horizontal perspective of the larger limbs that could hide a squirrel.

The oak was a big white oak, straight and strong. A few years later, when the camp was completely shut down, word would spread around that it had been sold. Surveyors came in and marked the woods with lengths of orange tape tied to wooden stakes driven into the earth. Soon after that, Danny and I would come here and find hundreds of the biggest oaks along this ridge marked with red slashes and bars spray-painted about chest high on the bark. A few trees with heavy storm damage or trunk cavities had NO CUT written on them. Knowing what was coming, one day we rearranged many of the stakes in a way that was meant to befuddle the surveyors so thoroughly that they'd abandon their project. The next morning we sneaked some red paint from the garage and went up to the ridge. Our paint didn't quite match the color used on the trees, but we went around writing NO CUT anyway.

It didn't help. A few months later they took out the oaks. Then, a year or so later, crews came in with heavy equipment and started clearing a network of roads. In the years after high school, at least a half dozen of my friends would build houses in what was once the Camp Woods. They'd put in square-shaped lawns of turf grass and their young kids would play in the very places where I used to hunt. Even though I'd resent my friends for this, I'd turn around and find work using a chain saw to clear building lots in other, not-too-distant patches of woods. Later still, I would look at that period of time as a form of madness that I not only endured but participated in.

But right now, as I looked for a squirrel that was bellying a limb, that future was unknown to me. I shifted around and viewed the tree from a variety of angles until I noticed a slight bulge on the top of a limb that didn't seem quite right. The bulge was against a backdrop of leaves. I moved back and forth a little in order to position the bulge in such a way that there was clear sky behind it. My suspicions were confirmed. Against the sky, the bulge on the limb had the slight halo-like appearance that occurs when sunlight shines through fur.

I leaned the barrel of my .22 against a trunk and used my right hand to stabilize it. When I squeezed the trigger the squirrel's body went instantly stiff and then it slid off the limb a bit. It hung there by four feet and then two feet and then one foot and then none. The array of complex emotions that would later come to me whenever I killed an animal for food—gratitude, reverence, guilt, indebtedness—were still years away from developing. Instead, I felt nothing but the pure joy of accomplishment when the squirrel hit the ground. I walked over to finish it off by cracking its skull with the sole of my moccasin. I was a hunter in the American wilderness, and that was good enough for now.

|||||||||||||||||||||||||||||||||||||||||||||||||||||||||||||||||||||||||||||||||||||||||||||||||||||||||||||||||||||||||||

Tasting Notes: Squirrel

It annoys me that "tastes-like-chicken" has become such a joke and cliché, because that really is a decent way of describing squirrel meat. Or at least it's pretty accurate in terms of the structural qualities of squirrel meat, such as texture, density, grain, and color. It's not as applicable when it comes to taste, but I can forgive people for thinking so. Many folks are only really familiar with the tastes of two kinds of meat. And since squirrel is completely different from beef, the field of potential comparisons is quickly whittled down to chicken.

I don't get excited about eating beef or chicken. It's not that I have any particular gripe against either, it's just that I prefer to eat game meat and I always keep a freezer full of the stuff. Most of this meat comes from large ungulates that fall under the "big-game" category, including whitetail deer, mule deer, moose, elk, and caribou. While these animals all look different and occupy different ecological niches, their meat tends to be remarkably similar. There are certainly some subtle differences between species and individual animals, but it's all pretty much red and lean.

Hands down, I would select this type of meat if someone ever put a gun to my head and made me choose a single kind of food to eat for the rest of my life. It really is that good, and good for you. However, a constant diet of lean red meat does have its drawbacks—namely that you start to fantasize about eating something besides lean red meat. That's where squirrel comes in handy. Its flesh has a pale translucency with an almost purplish tint. Soak it in a tub of salt water overnight in your fridge, which helps remove the blood and makes the meat even juicier, and it takes on a more pleasing whitish color. Over the years I've cooked squirrel in many good ways: dredged in flour and then browned in a pan and then braised in game stock; dredged in flour and then browned in a pan and then baked; marinated in water and cider vinegar, then browned and braised. Usually the flesh comes out the color of hot chocolate, but with a silky, rich quality to it. It does look a lot like the dark leg meat of a braised chicken.

When I was a kid, my mom would sometimes pack the legs and backs of eight or nine squirrels in her Crock-Pot and then submerge them in Campbell's cream of mushroom soup. (Nationally, I'd bet that millions of squirrels have been cooked this way over the years.) She'd let them cook all day on the medium setting. At some point during this process, the meat would begin to fall away from the bones. When we were done eating, we'd find all those bones settled on the bottom of the Crock-Pot, looking like the exhumed ancient mass graves in archaeological photos.

Now I like to cook my squirrels so that the meat stays on the bone, but just barely. Done properly it should pull away almost as easily as hot wings, though the meat of a squirrel tears a little differently. While a hot wing tends to tear apart according to the placement of your teeth, a squirrel leg tends to break apart according to muscle groups. Eating one can be a vivid lesson in anatomy. Using your teeth as carefully as a paring knife to disconnect and pull away a squirrel's calf muscle can leave you imagining the flesh beneath the skin of your own leg.

Sometimes I get such a craving for squirrel meat that I'll go to extremes to get it. My wife and I have an eight-hundred-square-foot vegetable garden behind our apartment in Brooklyn, New York. It's a squirrel hot spot. They're especially abundant in the late summer, when they show up by the dozen to steal my ripening tomatoes. While New York state has a regulated squirrel season (September 1–February 29 or November 1–February 29, depending on zone), you're obviously not allowed to discharge a .22 rifle within city limits. So what I've done in the past is set traps for them. Snap-type rat traps work, as do body-gripping traps intended for muskrats and mink. The method is of very questionable legality, but keep in mind that New Yorkers are prone to carpeting the perimeters of their homes and buildings with rat poison that is accessible to squirrels and no one gets riled up about that. So if you can get away with slowly killing animals with poison and then not eating them, I have to think that killing them instantly and consuming them is a morally superior position.

I skin the squirrels inside, over the sink. This is not totally to my wife's liking. She grew up, as I did, in Michigan, but her family did not hunt or own guns; in fact, Katie did not grow up with an entirely favorable impression of hunters. Through many subsequent experiences together, she's come to respect my passion as well as the constant supply of organic meat that it provides. She's now eaten more game meat than half of the hunters I know. Yet she still has no interest in killing an animal, and the skinning of squirrels in our kitchen makes her wonder what she got herself into by marrying me, and whether it's too late to get out of it. I like to remind her that we wouldn't have met if it wasn't for hunting, because she worked for the publisher of my first book on that subject. She reminds me that we wouldn't have met if it weren't for *not* hunting, because if she was a hunter she wouldn't have been living in New York and working in book publishing.

The last time I harvested two squirrels from beneath my tomato plants, I snipped them up the spine with kitchen shears and then cut them into quarters by severing each half between the flank and the rib cage. I mashed some coarse salt, fresh thyme, and garlic into a pulp in a mortar and pestle, and then wet that mixture with olive oil and the juice of a lemon. It's a recipe that I borrowed from the British chef Jamie Oliver, who probably does not trap too many squirrels. After piercing each quarter about a dozen times with a fork, I slathered them in the marinade and let them sit for a few hours. The meat then went on the grill, where it stayed until it was cooked well enough that I could pop the rear ball joints with a light twist.

My wife's displeasure with the origins and preparation of the meal faded as the squirrel made a slow and steady transition from critter to cuisine. She was pleasantly surprised when she ate it. It was dense and richly textured, not at all dry. I flashed her one of those I-told-you-so looks, which she returned with a smile.

"But let's not make a habit of this," she said. "I'm serious, Steve. You hear me?"

||||||||||||||||||||||||||||||||||||||||||||||||||||||||||||||||||||||||||||||||||||||||||||||||||||

CHAPTER THREE

Tangle Stake

★

I MIGHT NOT HAVE opened the box had I known that its contents would dominate my life for the next decade, but I had no way of seeing that coming. Instead my brothers and I ripped open the package to find six #1 long-spring traps made by Victor. These are muskrat-sized versions of leghold traps, which hold an animal by gripping its foot between two rounded steel jaws. They'd been sent by our mysterious half brother, Frank Rinella II, who was the same age as our mother. Since Frank II maintained only a sporadic relationship with our father, we didn't know much about him beyond the fact that he had taken an early retirement as a game warden in Colorado in order to become a full-time elk-hunting guide. That he'd already held the two coolest jobs in the world made him a hero in our minds. That he thought enough of us to send a present only added to his stature. To me, he was something like a cross between Daniel Boone and Santa Claus.

Regardless of who they came from, I would have accepted the traps with gratitude because their arrival coincided with a period of extremely high fur prices that is now known to trappers as the fur boom. Beginning around 1975 and lasting through 1986, the boom was driven by strong retail demand for many varieties of fur and fur-trimmed garments. The economy was generally good, people were hungry for outward manifestations of wealth and luxury, and fur provided that.*

Trappers were raking in money in a way they hadn't done since the Roaring Twenties. A single muskrat pelt could earn a trapper around seven or eight dollars, maybe more.† Raccoon hides brought up to forty dollars.‡ Mink could be worth fifty dollars.§ Coyotes, seventy dollars.‖ Fox, eighty dollars. Beaver, a hundred.# Suddenly you

---

*The popularity of fur had gotten so great that consumer demand defied logic. We're all familiar with the image of New York pimps wearing full-length furs in not-so-cold weather (which was a phenomenon that coincided with the beginning of the fur boom) and it extended to other demographics as well. During the boom, one of the largest furriers in the country was in Las Vegas, even though that city has average January highs of 58 degrees. Another peculiarity of the fur boom of the 1970s and '80s was that almost every species of furbearing animal experienced a sharp increase in value. Everything from opossums to wolves were bringing record highs. It's more common for just one or two species—or even varieties of species—to rise in value at any given time. Take bobcats, for instance. In the latter part of the first decade of the 2000s, bobcats from the western United States with white bellies and clearly defined black spots were bringing up to five or six hundred dollars apiece. At the same time, you could hardly get ten or twenty dollars for a sandy-bellied bobcat from the eastern United States.

†Muskrat furs from the United States were primarily sold domestically and to Western Europeans. They were used as a liner in outerwear, including rainwear. Bomber hats made of muskrat fur were also popular.

‡Raccoon pelts were commonly used for full-length coats. Generally, pelts from northern animals tend to outprice pelts from southern animals, because northern animals have thicker and heavier hides. But raccoons presented an anomaly to this rule because they were popular with Asian women. It is difficult to sell heavy furs to Asian women, because they generally have slighter frames. A nine-pound coat is about the limit. For this reason, thinly furred coats from southern raccoons were bringing higher prices than heavily furred northern raccoons. However, the market for northern raccoons was, at least in part, supported by Italian women—who will buy fur coats weighing eleven pounds.

§Mink was used for stoles, garment trim, and short and full-length coats and jackets.

‖Coyote, along with fox and bobcat, were regarded as "fun" furs by furriers. They were flashy, and particularly popular in places such as Colorado ski towns. Coyote furs were also used widely as trim on parka hoods. The best fur for this is wolverine, as the hollow hairs trap heat and do not collect frost from exhaled breath.

#Beaver pelts are commonly sheared to a velvet-like shortness and used in garments. They are sometimes bleached and dyed as well. You'll see advertisements for "sheared blonde beaver," which stretches the limits of double entendre. The most common application for beaver pelts is the production of wool felt from the fur. Wool felt made from beaver is water resistant and was highly prized as a material for men's top hats.

could make a living as a professional trapper, an occupation that hadn't been financially feasible in many decades. Prices were so high, in fact, that a lot of guys in my area tried their damnedest to get laid off from their regular jobs because they'd make more money trapping as long as they were able to supplement their fur money by collecting unemployment benefits. I remember a day when I was watching a local trapper and taxidermist skin his catch in his basement while he talked to a buddy over the phone. I couldn't tell if they were discussing competitors who'd moved in on their trapping territory, or if they were discussing a plan to move in on the territory of their competitors, but whichever it was, the trapper ended the discussion by saying, "Anyone fucks with you, shoot 'em." He seemed to be only half joking.

My brothers and I weren't yet looking to escape the drudgery of second-shift factory jobs, though it was easy to see that trapping muskrats could be way more profitable than mowing lawns. And way more romantic. For a kid in love with animals and the out-of-doors, it was possible to view the history of North America through fur-tinted lenses. Basically, the first guy to go just about anywhere on this continent was going there in search of animal pelts: Fur was on the brain of the otherwise gold-crazed Spaniards when they began poking around Florida and the Mississippi Delta and the Southwest and the California coast; Henry Hudson went up the Hudson River with an eye toward finding pelts; when the first load of exports left the Plymouth Colony at Massachusetts Bay in 1621, the bulk of its value was in

---

The demand for such hats lasted for many decades, and drove the market for beaver all through the colonial and frontier period of North American history. In the 1830s, the fashion shifted toward silk top hats, which killed the beaver felt market with a thoroughness and rapidity that brings to mind the way cassette tapes were slaughtered by compact disk technology in the early 1990s. Nowadays, cowboy hats made from beaver wool felt are still popular, and the wool is used for pool tables and card tables and such.

fur; Samuel de Champlain, the Father of New France (aka Canada) established the cities of Montreal and Quebec in part to facilitate the search for furs.*

In 1803, when Lewis and Clark headed up the Missouri River, they were under orders to investigate the feasibility of trading for furs with the tribes of the Great Plains and the Rockies. Their reports about the abundance of fur in the Rockies inspired some of the greatest feats in American history. Trapper Jed Smith was the first white man to cross the Great Basin and the Sierra Nevada and to enter California through an overland route. Trapper Jim Bridger was the first white man to visit the Great Salt Lake. John Colter became the first white man to ever pass through what eventually became Yellowstone National Park; for a long time, people were incredulous of Colter's reports and they referred to the place as Colter's Hell.

I felt as though I was reliving an important part of history when my brothers and I began scouting for muskrat sign in preparation for the opening day of muskrat trapping season on the first of November. Muskrats are members of the rodent family. An adult muskrat can weigh up to a few pounds and reach a length of twenty-four inches. Their fur is much more beautiful than anything you might imagine growing on an animal whose name includes the word *rat*. They have dense, wool-like underfur all over their body, ranging from a pale

---

*At a time, particularly during the 1700s and 1800s, Canada was basically owned and operated by a trapping and fur trading outfit called Hudson's Bay Company. It was commonly known as HBC, leading employees to joke that it stood for "Here Before Christ." In the late 1700s, the company shipped out enough beaver pelts every year to make a half-million hats. It maintained its own naval force. When the French and Indian War broke out between French colonies and British colonies in 1756, it was largely over access to the country's beaver hides. This was nothing new—for a hundred years, France and England had been using Native Americans to fight a proxy war over beaver pelts. Russians were prowling the coastlines of Alaska for fur beginning in the 1740s, and they kept at it until we bought the place in 1867. Part of their interest in selling the territory came from the fact that they'd grossly overharvested the fur and felt that the land was degraded in value.

tannish color on the belly to a deep chocolate brown on the back. When a muskrat's hide is in prime condition—usually from November to early spring—it sports a lush growth of long, silky guard hairs that make it a perfect material for garment trim and also an affordable stand-in for mink.*

Muskrats live in colonies, or family groups, of usually five or six animals. Their existence is centered on water. They thrive in big bodies of it, like the Mississippi River, yet a colony wouldn't think twice about living its entire existence in a pond the size of a backyard swim-

---

*The subjects of trapping and fur garments always make me think of a funny story. A year or two after the events described in this chapter, I gave a furrier eight muskrat pelts and a payment of sixty dollars in order to make me a custom fur bomber hat— the kind with fur on the outside and ear flaps that can be tied in a knot at the top of your head. I wanted one of the hats because they looked cool, and also because they were worn by bush pilots and Yukon gold rushers and other people I admired.

I must have been at the beginning of a growing spurt when the furrier measured my head, because by the time I got the hat in the mail it fit very snugly. Within a year, it was so tight that it pressed a deep red line across my forehead and gave me mild headaches whenever I wore it. Within two years, I could only wear it for about ten minutes or so until the pain was such that I had to remove it.

One might think that I would have returned the hat for resizing, or simply quit wearing it, but the former idea never occurred to me and the latter idea was preposterous because the hat had cost me a lot of money and looked really cool. So what I would do was wear it until it hurt, and then put it in my pocket until the pain subsided, and then put it back on again. This, no doubt, led to the hat's loss. One day I was trapping muskrats through the ice in the middle of the winter and reached into the pocket of my insulated bib overalls in order to remove the hat, but it was gone. I looked and looked, but I couldn't find it. I was bummed for weeks.

The next spring, long after I'd forgotten about the hat, I happened to be driving along on Blue Lake Road in a station wagon owned by a drifter I knew named Barefoot. As we were passing a marsh where I sometimes did some trapping through the ice, I looked off to the side of the road and saw a muskrat lying near the edge of a melting snowbank right where I usually parked. "Dead muskrat," I yelled. "Right there!" Barefoot slammed on his brakes and I jumped out to investigate the animal to see if it was in good enough shape to have commercial value. But when I reached my prize, I was surprised to see that it was not a muskrat. It was my hat. It was now tighter than ever, but since it was soaking wet I thought I could maybe stretch it out by wearing it. I withstood the discomfort only so long, and the hat found its way back into my pocket as Barefoot and I set beaver traps near a place called Cisco Bayou. At the end of the day, when I reached into my pocket to retrieve the hat, it was gone again. I haven't seen it since, but if it ever turns up you can bet that I'm going to have it professionally resized.

ming pool as long as there was plenty of food and the water was deep enough that it didn't freeze all the way to the bottom in the winter. They sleep and find shelter either in subterranean dens dug into the banks of streams and lakes, or inside lodges that they build from cattails and other vegetation. The lodges range in size from bushel baskets to restaurant-sized garbage cans. There was a shortage of suitable lodge-building plants in the lakes around my house, so the muskrats there generally relied on bank dens. A major obstacle in constructing a bank den is beach sand. It's hard for a muskrat to tunnel through sand, as it tends to collapse and it's easy for predators to dig them out and kill them from above. Almost all of the shorelines in my area were sandy to the point that you could dig into them with those cheap plastic beach trowels that they sell in gift shops.

But luckily for the muskrats (and luckily for us), the early eighties had been pretty wet in our area. Water levels in the lakes had risen so high that the water had inundated the reed beds and lawn grass and weeping willow roots along the shorelines. The roots of the vegetation helped stabilize the den entrances of the muskrats and gave them almost unlimited habitat. And since a female can produce a couple dozen offspring in a single year, the population was at a peak just around the time we got our traps.

In fact, muskrats lived just fifty yards from my bedroom window. We had them underfoot, often literally. They liked to dig beneath our seawall and then excavate labyrinthine networks of subterranean tunnels under our yard. You'd be mowing the grass and your foot would bust through a hole in the ground and there'd be a nest down there lined with muskrat food: the roots and stems of milfoil, lily pad, cattail, and reeds; the shattered shells of clams and snails. When I got done mowing, I might jump into the lake for a swim. I liked to swim out to our floating raft very stealthily, so that I didn't scare away the muskrats that denned inside the raft's framework of wood and Styrofoam. That way, I could climb up onto the raft and jump on it in order to spook the muskrats out. Then I'd dive in after them and see how far I could chase them underwater before I had to come up for air.

In the weeks leading up to the official muskrat opener, my brothers and I scoured the area's shorelines in canoes and on bikes and by walking. We scouted on Middle Lake, where we lived, and also to the north, on North Lake; to the west, on West Lake; and to the east, on Twin Lake. Sometimes our mom drove us to look at ponds and lakes that were farther away. We found muskrat tracks in the sand, birdlike but with faint drag marks from the tail running between them; we found muskrat feed beds, dinner-plate-sized mats of vegetation built in sheltered locations where the muskrats felt safe from avian predators; and we found entrances to bank dens, revealed by yellow strips of sand where the passing traffic of muskrats had cleared away the muck so that it looked like a miniature version of a swimming area out in front of a frequently used beach.

We located so many muskrats that we figured we needed to make a capital investment in order to buy six Victor 110 Conibears in order to complement the six #1 legholds that we already owned.* Also known as body-grippers or killer-type traps, Conibears perform in a way that brings to mind a boa constrictor made of thin steel bars. They're ideally suited for the entrances of muskrat bank dens. The traps cost almost four dollars apiece, which we had to borrow from our old man. We all signed on the loan, the first that any of us had ever taken. By doing so, we became trappers in debt, and thus we joined that rare and adventurous class of men who have given so much rugged flavor to American history. Most of my heroes sprang into the wilderness—and into the history books—by exploring the

---

*Like doughnuts, eggs, and beer, traps are most commonly sold by the dozen and trappers discuss them in terms of dozens. Beyond tradition, I have no idea why this is the case. But I'd like to know.

country's wildest locations while financed by backers who were will-ing to gamble on the idea that a man could strike it rich on furs in the American wilderness. During Boone's trapping adventures in Appa-lachia he was often indebted (sometimes to an overwhelming degree) to a man named Richard Henderson. For a while, Jim Bridger and Jed Smith both operated on the finances of General William Ashley. John Colter, the veteran of the Lewis and Clark expedition, found financ-ing from a man named Manuel Lisa.

My dad jotted down the details of the loan on a yellow legal pad and explained that the money was due when we sold our first year's worth of fur. It's unlikely that my old man found any excitement in joining the ranks of history's trapping investors; instead, I think he was probably just pleased to offer opportunities to his children. Some dads give their kids new cars or send them to expensive schools as a form of compensation for things that they themselves never had as kids. My dad lent us money for traps.

He was born on the South Side of Chicago in 1924, a place and time when searching for muskrats would have seemed as far-fetched as searching for a Wi-Fi signal. His mother was a Czechoslovakian drinker named Juanita who'd go on benders that usually began with her sipping from liquor bottles customarily offered as an enticement to clients in the local drugstores. His father, Anthony Rinella, worked in the asphalt business and walked with a limp because he'd been shot in the leg during the race riots of 1919.

My dad told me several times that his first memory was of himself standing next to a high chair and holding its leg while his parents screamed at each other. They broke up when he was four. For reasons that I've never understood, and that he never attempted to explain, they were unwilling or unable to take care of him. One day his mother dropped him off at his father's parents' house on West Twenty-seventh Street and that's where he spent the rest of his childhood. His grandparents were Italian immigrants and spoke their native language in the home. His grandfather hauled produce in the city using a horse and wagon. It was my dad's job at night to brush and feed the horse and put him in his stable. His grandfather died when he was ten, and the body spent three days in the living room before going into the ground.

My dad's grandmother was volatile and would spank him with the bread paddles that she used for baking. After breaking a paddle over his backside, she'd make him go to the barn and fashion a replacement from the quarter-inch-thick wooden slats used in produce crates. My dad never saw her in any kind of clothes except black dresses. When her husband died, she was already in the process of mourning her son Phillip. He'd been shot dead when he was twenty-eight by an Irish American police officer named Toomey. The murder happened on a Monday night when Phillip pulled his '29 Ford Model A into the path of Toomey's '28 Model A. There was an argument, and Toomey pulled a .38 revolver and shot Phillip twice through the back.* My dad's grandmother retained his bloodied outfit and stored

*There was a brief investigation. In a *Chicago Evening American* article titled "Policeman Faces Writ in Killing," the journalist describes a moment when my grandfather Anthony personally questioned Toomey during an inquest. He asked, "Why did you shoot when my brother was running away?" Toomey responded, "I thought he was going to shoot me." As a punishment Toomey was suspended, without pay, for one week. I have the original newspaper clipping about my great-uncle Phillip's murder/shooting. The clip measures two inches by nine inches, and it's so old that it's taken on the color of cardboard. The layout of the newspaper is such that there is a complete article on the back side of the clipping titled "German Dye Trust To Sell Movie Interests." It explains how I. G. Farben, the giant German chemical and dye conglomerate, was getting out of the movie industry by liquidating its film production company and ceasing to be the distributor of United Artists' films in Germany. The article cites uncertain conditions in the German movie industry as the reason. This company would later work hand in hand with the Nazis during World War II, which became my father's war. I. G. Farben advised the Nazis on which chemical plants to seize during the invasions of Czechoslovakia and Poland. They used slave laborers at Auschwitz to produce synthetic oil and rubber. And they held the patent for—as well as manufactured, labeled, and distributed—the cyanide-based pesticide known as Zyklon B. This it in a paper box on the top shelf of a hall closet. My dad pulled it down to inspect it often, and liked to put his fingertip through the bullet holes.

The Great Depression hit when my dad was five. Besides dashing what had been a long stretch of high fur prices spurred by the fashion trends of the Roaring Twenties, it dashed his family's meager finances. My father earned small change hauling contraband liquor from house to house by concealing it beneath a blanket in a wagon. At night he'd go to the freight yard to gather pieces of heating coal that fell off railcars. When he couldn't find any, he might climb onto a train and help some fall. Back then there was a decent market for used cotton materials. He stole shop rags from the maintenance department of a nearby foundry that produced horseshoes by reaching through the windows to grab oiled rags from a steel drum. One time he turned around from the window to find a revolver in his face.

The Japanese bombed Pearl Harbor when he was seventeen and he dropped out of school to work on a defense plant assembly line. His job was to cut the grooves into castellated nuts. He enlisted with the army when he turned eighteen. He was assigned to the army's 87th Infantry Division and was sent to basic training in Grenada County, Mississippi. Before he was sent overseas, a girl he'd been seeing in Chicago showed up in Mississippi. She was carrying a baby in her belly and a wedding ring in her hand. He married her, his first wife, in a courthouse. The army then shipped my dad to Casablanca, Morocco, where he was stationed at what he referred to as a "repo depot" (repo meaning "replacement," as in fresh troops to be processed). From there men were assigned to divisions that had been

---

product of theirs was used to exterminate Jews in concentration camps, including, presumably, many of the same eighty-three thousand slave laborers they put to work in their factories. My dad always referred to Germans (the ones who lived in Germany, that is) as "Krauts," and he had a hard time letting go of his distrust and hatred for them.

stripped of soldiers due to the massive casualties of the North African campaign.

Somehow, through all of that, my father managed to develop a deep love for the outdoors and hunting even though no one in his family had ever done that—at least not since arriving in America. My dad told me stories of hopping railroad cars out into the farm country outside Chicago. He'd sleep beneath a canvas tarp in the brushy strips of woods along the tracks, and he'd catch fish out of stream culverts that ran beneath the tracks. In the city, he'd spend days on the Chicago piers fishing for yellow perch and selling his catch to passersby. When he thought about his early passion for the outdoors, he liked to say it was in his DNA, because where else would it have come from? Considering that modern humans have spent well over 90 percent of their history as hunters and fishermen, there was probably a bit of truth in his assessment. We were built to follow game, capture it, and butcher it. The fact that his kids might make some spending money in such a way seemed to him to be perfectly normal and acceptable.

As the opening day of muskrat season approached, my brothers and I jumped into our new pastime with fanatical intensity. We hung out our traps in the rain so they'd get a light coat of rust on them, and then we boiled them in a galvanized tub set over a fire and filled with water, oak bark, and husks from black walnuts that we collected in the woods and smacked open with sledgehammers. The traps came out brownish black. We then dipped them in melted paraffin wax in order to make them slick and fast. By law, traps must have the owner's name affixed to them. At night, we cut strips of aluminum from beer cans and etched our names and license numbers into the metal with an awl. We used brass wire to fix the tags to the chains on the traps. On Halloween, the day before opening day, we rode our bikes to the end of Dead Dog Road* and used machetes to cut a small bundle of four-foot-long poplar poles. Sharpened on one end, these would be used to anchor our traps to the lake bed so that the muskrats didn't haul them off when they got caught. Our dad took some pop rivets and a roll of canvas webbing and fitted a five-gallon bucket with shoulder straps so we could carry all our gear around. We punched some holes in the bottom so that water would drain out. We then loaded it up: traps, a hatchet and machete, a tube of mint toothpaste, Q-tips, a canvas coin bag full of nails and wire staples.

When a trapper heads out to place his traps, he's said to be laying out a line. The thinking on this is that the traps are like waypoints along a route—the trapline—that the trapper will follow whenever he visits his traps to remove animals and make necessary adjustments. We left home during the final moments of Halloween day, so that we'd be in position to begin setting traps when the season opened at the turn of midnight.

Our promptness was inspired by general excitement, and also by a fear of competition. For weeks we'd been sweating the idea that some rival trapper would swoop in and snatch our muskrats out from underneath us. To defend against competition, we decided to set our first trapline along North Lake. We figured it was most vulnerable to interlopers because it was less developed than Middle Lake, the one

---

*That wasn't the real name of the road, but we called it that because there was a spell of time when you could pretty reliably find dead dogs in the ditches and roadside marshes along there. Because we did not recognize the dogs as neighborhood pets, we suspected that they were feral dogs that had been shot for the crime of running deer. (Now, looking back on this, I wonder if the road commission workers weren't just using this area as a dumping ground for road-killed dogs.) Since the subject of dead dogs has come up a couple of times in this book already, I'm motivated here to explain that I've never killed or harmed a dog, though I have eaten dog meat on several occasions in another country. As for feral cats, another great killer of game and songbirds, my relationship to them hasn't been so passive.

we lived on, and therefore might seem more inviting and accessible to guys who didn't live around there.

An individual trap and its context on the ground or in the water are known collectively as a set. There are many, many varieties of trapping sets, though they are generally organized into two categories: bait sets and blind sets. Bait sets rely on olfactory attractants or visual stimulants to lure the animal toward the trap.* Blind sets are placed in the path that an animal might naturally use without provocation or enticement—though you can influence the animal's specific line of travel with small sticks or other obstacles without forfeiting the blind set classification.

On our first night of muskrat trapping, we used what basically amounted to blind sets even though we placed the Q-tips dipped in mint toothpaste near some of the traps because we'd read that muskrats liked the smell. Our six Conibears went into den entrances. Making these sets was so easy you could hardly mess it up. The holes usually have a concave, troughlike runway, called a "run," leading up to them. These runs are usually about the same width as a 110 Conibear—or, rather, 110 Conibears are made to be about the same width as these runs. Say about six inches. If the run's not wide enough

---

*Such attractants and stimulants, known as "lures," might include bird's wings (for catching bobcat); slightly spoiled meat, or fresh meat (for fox, coyote, skunk, opossum, etc.); fresh, oily varieties of fish (for raccoon, mink, otter); edible plants such as poplar and cattail (for beaver, muskrat); animal urine (for most furbearing animals, depending on the urine used); and homemade or commercially produced lures that are usually made from liquefied or oil-based blends of pulverized glands, skunk essence, beaver castor, and extracts of fish and meat. (As with urine, they make lure blends that are attractive to just about every furbearing animal.) I used to make my own lure blend for fox, raccoon, and coyote. It was a mixture of beaver castor, a touch of molasses, a dash of fish oil, and the hunks of flesh and rendered oil from feral cats that I'd butcher and bury in the ground in Mason jars until they were partially rotten, or as we'd say, "tainted." I'd then stabilize the concoction with glycerin in order to halt the rot.

to accommodate the trap, you can widen it by digging it out with a machete or hatchet. Or else you just stuff the toe of your boot in there and wiggle it around and widen it out until the trap fits. We soon learned to call this "bootin' out a run." If the run is too wide, you just funnel it down with some guide sticks shoved into the bottom. We called that "neckin' down a run." Once the Conibear was in place, we'd run a stake through the ring on the trap's chain and shove it into the bottom of the lake.

I'll always remember the last trap we set that night. It was on a peninsula of land that we called Crazy Mary's Point, in honor of a mean old lady who had supposedly hanged herself in an old cottage nearby. There was a muskrat den on the eastern edge of the peninsula, but the runway was positioned right beneath a submerged log. There was no room beneath this log for a Conibear trap. The three of us got into a big argument over what to do. Either move the log and make room for the trap, or try to slip a foothold trap beneath the log and see if that worked. While Danny supported the latter idea, Matt and I supported the former. We argued about this for some time, keeping it to whispers because we were on Crazy Mary's Point and that seemed like the right thing to do. Eventually Danny won out, on the grounds that moving the log would spook the muskrats that lived there. So he lay out on the log, dangling his arm in the water while he felt around in the underwater darkness for the perfect place to set the foothold. I remember being overcome by a great sense of pride in being his brother, because reaching into dark water where you couldn't see anything was scary business.

A Conibear will kill a muskrat pretty much outright, but a leghold won't. You need to rig the trap so that the muskrat drowns, or else it might twist off its leg and get away. To do this in shallow water requires various tricks, depending on the circumstances. We took about a body's length of fourteen-gauge wire and wrapped one end around the ring of the trap's chain and wrapped the other end around a stake that we drove into the mud in about two feet of water. Next, we pounded in another stake about three feet beyond that, in even deeper water. This was called a tangle stake. The muskrat would swim out and get the trap's wire all tangled up, and then he wouldn't be able to come back into the shallows. The concept is sort of similar to when you're walking a leashed dog and he passes on the opposite side of a tree from you, except there's no person around to help the muskrat get sorted back out again.*

With our work done, we walked back home.

Looking back on it, I think that that night—the wee hours of November 1, 1984—was the first night of my life that I did not sleep at all. I was way too excited. My head swarmed with thoughts of success and failure, riches and poverty, and my dreams of being a modern-day frontiersman. I was also troubled by a deal that I'd struck with my brothers about the next day. The deal had to do with the fact that Danny and Matt were in seventh and eighth grades, respectively, and that their school was pretty far away. They had a half-mile walk to the bus stop and then a forty-five-minute bus ride, which meant that they had to leave before sunup. This, in turn, meant that they wouldn't be able to run our trapline until after they got home from school, as we didn't want to disturb it in the early morning predawn hours while the muskrats were in their peak period of activity. I, on the other hand, was still in fifth grade, and my school was just two miles away and I always rode my bike there unless there was too much snow. So, knowing that I'd have plenty of time to check some of the traps in the

*Believe me, I realize that it would be appropriate to address the brutality of all this. But there's really nothing I can say that would make it more palatable. As much as I hate the expression, it is what it is.

morning on my own, Matt and Danny made me promise that I wouldn't.

I want to clarify here that my two brothers are among the few most important people in my life. I've been in the company of at least one of them on about 90 percent of the occasions when something truly memorable has happened to me in the woods, and I love them in a way that would not make sense if I tried to write it out. There are no words for it, no sentences good enough. With that said, I have to confess a secret that I've kept from them for the past twenty-eight years. After Matt and Danny left for school on Thursday, November 1, 1984, I crumbled under the great anxiety and excitement that comes with being a fledgling muskrat trapper. I'm not proud of this, but it's true. If I have any excuse at all, it's only that one of my most common routes to school roughly paralleled North Lake's southern bank. The temptation was too much to withstand, so rather than riding down the road on my bike, I walked it down the steep blueberry-covered hill behind the Babcock family's house and came to the shore of the lake. I kept to dry ground while I pushed my bike along the lakeshore toward the first trap, so that my bike tires didn't leave any traces in the mud that would betray my betrayal.

As I got close, maybe about twenty yards away, I noticed a strange black shape, like an eight-inch chunk of rope, floating next to the stake. It sat at the top of the lake in the way bull kelp will float near the surface of the ocean when the tide is out. A couple of steps later and I could see that the rope was actually a muskrat tail, and that one end of it was attached to the submerged and furry rump of a muskrat that was clenched in the jaws of the Conibear. I didn't even touch the muskrat. Instead I ran down the shoreline toward the next stake. The next trap was empty, and I passed by without stopping. I then passed several more empty ones, and my enthusiasm started to fade. But just as I approached the point of land near Crazy Mary's Point I passed a weeping willow where we'd set a Conibear in a bank den entrance that was burrowed between two tree roots. Again I was greeted by the black snaky tail of a muskrat gripped in the trap.

I ran on past, my eyes now focused on the stake that we'd placed where Danny had reached under the log. I had a sinking feeling when I didn't see a tail there, but something still looked kind of strange to me. I could see the wire running out toward the depths. I peered into the murky water, trying to decipher what I was seeing. Then it came to me. Out there, under the water and wrapped around the tangle stake, was a drowned muskrat. He was as big as the other two put together. If it wasn't an eight-dollar muskrat, I figured that nothing was. And while I would later catch more than a thousand furbearing animals in my trapping career, and I would pull as many as

Danny (right) helps me show off our first muskrat. Hundreds more would follow.

twenty-seven muskrats in a single day and as many as 250 muskrats in a single month, catching that big muskrat was for a long time the pinnacle of my happiness and clarity as a trapper. It inspired me to jump and whoop, something that probably hadn't happened in a long time on Crazy Mary's Point.

As I cut up the hill and hit Duff Road and pedaled toward school, I knew that three things in my life had changed. First, I knew that I wouldn't lie to my brothers ever again because I was really starting to dread having to recheck the traps with them while pretending to be surprised by the outcome. Second, I would never again attend school on the opening day of trapping season, because I could see that formal education was too much of a distraction from my true calling. Third, I knew that I would make my living as a trapper for the rest of my life, no matter what I had to do.

The fulfillment of the first of those proclamations just came naturally. The second proclamation was easy to accomplish as well, because one of my father's favorite quotes was Mark Twain's line about not letting school interfere with your education. The third proclamation would prove to be much more difficult to achieve, and my attempts at its fulfillment would lead me to compromise and endanger just about everything I thought I believed in.

||||||||||||||||||||||||||||||||||||||||||||||||||||||||||||||||||||||||||||||||||||||||||||||||||||||||||||||

Tasting Notes: Beaver

Any book about the old trappers and mountain men from the 1800s will include a passage about their favorite food, beaver tails. Historians just can't help themselves from throwing this tidbit into any treatment on the subject, probably because it has a little shock value and also works to demonstrate the tenacity, resourcefulness, and hardscrabble appeal of that particular breed of men. And while it's unclear whether eating beaver tail was pervasive enough back then to support the historical emphasis on beaver tail writing today, one thing is certain: Anyone who reads about old trappers will at some point find himself wondering what, exactly, beaver tail tastes like.

My two brothers, Matt and Danny, were the first two people I ever knew who tried it. Or, at least, they *almost* tried it. Matt was going to Ferris State University in Big Rapids, Michigan, and he lived outside of town on Chippewa Lake. This was an area with lots of public land, and I'd go up there in late December and early January and base myself out of his house while trapping beaver through the ice. At night I would skin the animals on newsprint laid out over the kitchen's linoleum floor. I'd place the unfleshed hides in contractor bags and put them in the freezer, and then I'd suspend the castor sacs over a heater vent with cotton twine so they'd dry out. Having removed everything with good cash value from the beavers, I'd set the carcasses outside the front door to freeze. From there they'd get used as bait, or maybe I'd sell them for a few dollars to a musher who liked to feed them to his sled dogs on the day before a big race.

One night Matt and Danny were sitting around drinking beer when they got to wondering about the tails. They went out and removed one with a knife, and then took it inside to have a look. The tail resembled something you might find under a rock in a tide pool: black, scaly, and just about the thickness of a big man's hand and the length of two hands put end to end. It was not immediately obvious what part to eat. Looking at it from the severed end, they could see a compressed, oblong circle of scaly skin surrounding a core of whitish material resembling the gristle on beefsteak. That gristly stuff must have been what those mountain men were after, reasoned Matt. Old accounts always mention trappers roasting the tails next to smoldering campfires, but Matt and Danny figured that an oven ought to work even better. They laid the tail on a sheet of aluminum foil and tossed it in at 350 degrees. A while later the oven was smoking and the tail was sizzling; they pulled it out to find that the scales had begun to peel off in a burned and grotesque way that reminded them of charred skin. They each ventured a nibble or two, and later notified me that it tasted like gristle though you couldn't really chew it.

That experience got us to thinking that the historians had screwed up. Since there was no way that mountain men were eating the actual tails of beavers, we concluded that "tail" must refer to the tail end, or rear of a

Me with a large beaver pulled from the ice near Big Rapids, Michigan.

beaver. Soon Matt and I were in his kitchen in the early morning, stuffing the back third of a skinned-out beaver into a slow cooker before we headed out for a day's trapping. We filled any cracks or crevices left in the pot with chopped onions, carrots, and potatoes, and then topped it off with water and a sprinkling of salt and pepper. Eight hours later, we were greeted at his home by a dish with the texture of pot roast and the taste of beef that's been perfumed with castor. It was splendid. And so ended the mystery, or so I thought.

Now I cringe at how many times I've corrected people who mentioned that mountain men ate beaver tails. "No they didn't," I'd say. "They were eating the back legs, like the tail *end*." I kept this up for at least a couple of years. Then I happened to be reading yet another account about mountain men that included a litany of specific beaver tail references that could hardly be confused. "Their [beaver] meat is very palatable," wrote a man who visited an encampment of mountain men in the Rockies in 1839. "The tails," he continued, "which are fat all through, are especially regarded as delicacies." Another man had this to say: "The beaver possesses great strength in his tail, which is twelve or fifteen inches long, four broad, and a half inch thick. This part of the animal is highly esteemed by trappers, and assimilates a fish in taste, though it is far superior to any of the finny tribe."

By this time, however, I had quit trapping. As much as I wanted to reassess the beaver tail situation, I was woefully short on beaver. My chance didn't arrive until a decade later, when I happened to be camped in a cave in Wyoming. According to local legend, the famous prospector and cannibal Alferd Packer had camped in this same cave in the late 1800s after allegedly murdering and eating some of his travel mates in Colorado. On this night I finally happened to have in my possession the tail of a freshly dead beaver that I'd caught in a snare earlier that morning. I built a fire and then cut a willow switch down along the creek and pierced the beaver's tail onto a sharpened end. I wedged the other end of the switch into a crack in the rock near the fire so that the tail hung about twelve inches from the flame. I let it hang there for almost an hour, and reached over now and then to rotate the tail with a multi-tool. First, the scaly skin got kind of bubbly. Next, the skin started to get crispy and thin, almost like the skin of a baked potato. Finally, the skin started to pull away to reveal the shiniest and nicest block of fat that you've ever laid eyes on. It resembled what you might find on the edge of a fat beefsteak.

I sliced away a shaving, as thin as a slice of prosciutto. The fat melted in my mouth like butter, leaving a gristly bit of leftover that felt like a combination of beef jerky and Styrofoam. It was wonderful. I had another slice. And another. Perhaps my enthusiasm for the beaver tail was nourished by the fact that I was camped in a cannibal's lair and I didn't want to be upstaged, but I really did like it. After eating, I went out to the mouth of the cave with my flashlight and looked around for the weird bits of mysteriously human-like bone that had supposedly littered the entrance at some forgotten time. Looking back in, I surveyed the corner of the cave where I had sat to eat the beaver's tail. It was pretty much the only comfy spot there, and it was easy to imagine the old cannibal Alferd reclining there during his own mealtimes. What a world, I thought. What a strange and oddly edible world.

|||||||||||||||||||||||||||||||||||||||||||||||||||||||||||||||||||||||||||||||||||||||||||||||||

CHAPTER FOUR

Low and to the Right

★

B Y FAR, THE most popular kind of hunting story that exists today is the first-deer story. To kill your first deer is a rite of passage, and a hunter will tell his story with the same degree of passion and mystery that most guys use to describe their first sexual encounter. Indeed, there are many similarities between these two milestones in a boy's (and in some cases, a girl's) life. For instance, American hunters generally kill their first deer around the age that they begin fondling members of the opposite sex, say around fourteen or fifteen years of age. Also, our parents tend to respond to the news of our conquests in similar ways. Our dads take a quiet pride in our accomplishment. And while our mothers certainly don't want too many graphic details, they do begin to worry about what we might carry home with us.

If we continue this comparison, it's easy to see why so few hunters discuss the first time that they *didn't* get a deer. Who wants to tell—or hear, for that matter—a story about failed conquest? But for whatever reason, I think about the first deer that I didn't kill about ten times as often as I think about the first deer that I did kill. Even though I was only twelve years old, I can still see that deer—a four-point* whitetail

*Eastern count, that is. In the West, hunters describe a four-point buck as a two-pointer, as they only count the number of tines on a single antler. (An eight-point in the East would be a four-point out West; a twelve in the East, a six out West.) Personally, I

buck—as clearly as if he'd walked in front of me a week ago. I remember the slight curve of his antlers. I remember how his head bobbed downward and forward a little bit with each step. And I remember how the muscles in his front left shoulder flexed as he walked, and how, every time they flexed, you could see one of his veins bulge beneath his skin, the way you can see the shape of a garden hose lying in your backyard after a bit of snow has fallen on it. Looking at that shoulder, I thought of the directions that my old man had been pounding into my head for the past year: Sink your arrow an inch behind the shoulder, about a third of the way up the deer's body, and you've got a heart-shot buck. And though I had been perfectly willing—even excited—to do that, I knew now that I couldn't. Worse, I knew that I'd have to explain why.

Make the classic mitten-shaped Michigan map with your right hand, palm facing you, and look to the middle knuckle of your ring finger. That's Lake County, right where this buck lived. I grew up about fifty miles to the south and west of there, in Muskegon County, where the base of your pinkie meets the base of your ring finger. Hunting this far from home was a rare thing for me. It happened only when I was able to take time away from school in order to go on overnighters with my dad. Committing to such a thing was a huge gamble, as you were exposing yourself to the risk of one of his explosive freak-outs. These could be caused by the usual stuff, like if you back-talked him.

---

prefer the western system because it provides a better way of describing bucks with asymmetrical tine numbers. Say you've got a buck with four tines on its left antler and six tines on its right antler. An eastern hunter would describe this as a "ten-pointer" or a "nontypical ten," while a western hunter might just call it a "four by six." Because I hunt in the East and the West, and have friends in each, I usually avoid ambiguity and describe all bucks using the lingo that western hunters reserve for asymmetrical animals: two by twos, two by threes, three by threes, four by fives, six by sixes.

And they could also happen for strange and less predictable reasons, like, for instance, if you spilled pickle juice in his truck, or tracked dirt into the tent, or lost some gear, or snagged him on the top of the head with a fishing hook. All in all, though, it was definitely worth the risk. Not only was there the opportunity of seeing new country and having exciting adventures; there was also the chance of meeting some of the eccentric characters that my old man counted among his hunting and fishing buddies.

One of his favorite eccentric buddies was a man named Eugene Groters. Groters lived in the northwest corner of Lake County, in Peacock Township. He wore his reddish hair as a flat-topped buzz cut, and his wrist was permanently stained green from a large copper bracelet that he believed to be an effective treatment against arthritis. He liked to wear his pants high up on his waist, at a point well past his navel. If he'd been more limber, he could have probably reached over his shoulder and grabbed his wallet out of his back pocket. The pants were held in place by large red suspenders, which he wore with such consistency that I imagined him sleeping in them—a strange image considering that Groters kept a large mirror fastened to the ceiling above his bed well into the sixth decade of his life.

Groters maintained a collection of vintage *Playboy* centerfolds from the early days of that magazine's history—a time when *Playboy* offered images no more shocking than what you can find nowadays on the cover of *Us Weekly*. He kept them stapled to the walls of his barn. He was an enthusiastic fixer of broken mechanical contraptions, and he liked to invent mechanical contraptions that would soon break. He kept a lot of oddities and junk around as a source of inspiration and raw material. Some of these oddities were on permanent display in his cabin: a pair of twin deer fetuses preserved in a jar of formaldehyde; a dried bull's scrotum; an assortment of antique traps; and a knife that he claimed had been used on one of the Apollo

Eugene Groters gives some marksmanship pointers to my brother Matt.

lunar missions. The centerpiece of this archive was formed by Groters's collection of rifles and shotguns. He bragged of having one for every year he'd been alive, which made for a considerable arsenal.

Groters didn't like bow hunters. He referred to them as Hiawathas, a term that was meant to emasculate and trivialize practitioners of the discipline. By Groters's reckoning, hunting deer with a bow was little more than a good way to injure a deer. His opinion was backed by vivid personal and semipersonal experience. He had once shot a deer that had an infected wound from an arrowhead that was buried in its flesh, and he had visited a wild game butcher who showed him a coffee can full of arrowheads that he'd pulled out of deer carcasses that rifle hunters had killed and brought in. That was all Groters needed to see, and from then on he considered wounded and unrecovered deer to be the hallmark of bow hunting. In his mind, the only acceptable way to kill a deer was with a high-powered rifle. He killed one that way every year, using a .30–30, often dropping it dead in its tracks.

Groters's opinions rubbed my dad the wrong way. The old man considered himself to be a bow hunter, first and foremost. He was an active supporter of an archery organization known as the Pope and Young Club, and he hunted everything from bullfrogs to boars with his bow. He'd even met and hunted with the legendary Fred Bear, one of the pioneers of modern bow hunting.* Whenever my dad cared to explain the efficacy of bow hunting, he produced from his bookshelves the skull of a whitetail doe he'd killed near his old hunting cabin in Wisconsin. The skull had been penetrated by a steel arrowhead smack in the middle of its forehead, and then the arrowhead had buried itself so deeply into the back of the skull that the tip was poking into the light of day on the other side. This was done with an old recurve bow at forty yards, he reminded you, not some modern compound. Never mind that my dad's shot placement on the doe had been a complete accident—he was actually aiming for the deer's heart, but the animal had whipped its head around upon hearing the release of the bowstring and thereby caught the projectile between its eyes. He still cited the skull as testament to what a bow could do in the right hands. To bolster his case even further, he talked about a guy he served with in World War II who was hit in the forehead by a bullet that skirted around the top of his skull and exited out of his scalp without so much as fracturing the bone. The implication being, of course, that a damned *rifle* couldn't always do what a bow could do.

Groters and the old man were both too old and ornery to have their opinions changed, so they'd found a mature way to avoid con-

---

*I count as one of my primary claims to fame the fact that Fred Bear bought me lunch in Akron, Ohio, when I was a little kid.

frontation: My dad was allowed to stay at Groters's cabin if he was fishing in the area, but he had to stay out in the woods in his tent if he was bow hunting. This arrangement seemed fairly black-and-white, but it left an interesting area of gray with regard to me and my dad's visit on the occasion that I didn't kill the buck. We were planning to come to Lake County a few days before the October 1 opening of archery season in order to do some scouting, which meant we'd be there at the same time that the king salmon were in the rivers. My dad figured that we could do some fishing in conjunction with our scouting. Groters would join us in the fishing, of course, though it threatened to put him in an uncomfortable position, since our fishing was auxiliary to our primary mission of scouting our bow-hunting locations.

Luckily for Groters and my father, the practice of scouting for deer was not necessarily exclusive to other activities. It's quite possible to scout for deer in such a way that it looks and feels like you're doing

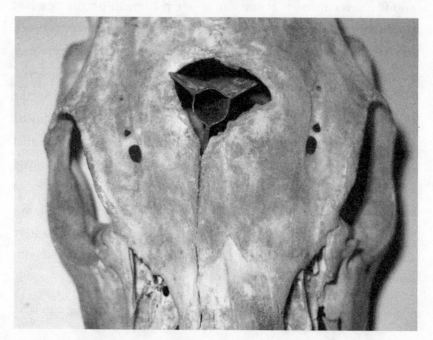

The doe's skull, showing the arrow's point of impact.

something else altogether. And in our case, that "something else" happened to be something that Groters usually insisted on doing at the end of a morning of fishing anyway. He liked to crack a can of Schlitz and take a circuitous backwoods route toward home. Along the way, he paid visits to a scattering of old burned-out houses in the woods that he believed to have been whorehouses back during the railroad boom of the 1920s. As evidence to support his theory, he would point to the profusion of bed frames and bedsprings that littered the inside and outside of these houses. Also the great abundance of old liquor bottles. He liked to stand and stare at these houses, and to feel the bottles in his hand, as though he could conjure through force of imagination the good times that had been had there. His love of the past went beyond simple nostalgia. He was also something of a preservationist. He took pleasure and pride in destroying any No Trespassing sign he encountered, with the justification that it hadn't been there before. In his mind, the signs were vagrant acts of graffiti.

These jaunts usually included some or all of Teapot Trail, a sandy two-track through the woods that allegedly took its name from a dented metal teapot that had once been nailed to a tree near the trail's intersection with a county dirt road. Over the decades, the pot was shot to shreds by guys armed with a wide array of rifles and shotguns before it finally vanished. Someone later came by and nailed a replacement to the tree, but Groters considered the new pot to have the same relationship to the original that a Rolling Stones tribute band has to the Rolling Stones.

Teapot Trail was prime deer country. That it ran through Manistee National Forest made it even better. It was public land, open to anyone who cared to hunt it, and there was no need to beg for permission. We scouted Teapot Trail by keeping the windows of our Jeep down and watching the sand for scatterings of deer tracks. When we saw them, we'd pull the truck to the side of the trail and go off into the woods to see what factors contributed to the presence of the deer in that particular area. These usually included some combination of trails, feeding areas, bedding areas, or geographical features that funneled traveling deer through the area. The first half of this process—driving with the windows down—dovetailed perfectly with Groters's own plan. And since he was generally curious about deer trails and geographical features, the second part didn't bother him too much so long as we didn't discuss bow hunting with too much specificity.

On or around the morning of September 28, we were driving slowly down Teapot Trail when we cut a bunch of deer tracks in the sand that alerted us to a game trail we'd never noticed before. We got out and I watched the old man study the tracks. They were of varying vintages, and only one size. No fawn tracks, no evidence of multiple deer crossing all at once. This led him to believe that a lone buck had been crossing the trail on a daily basis. We obliterated the tracks by sweeping the sand with a pine bough. The next morning, when we drove through that area an hour before daybreak on our way to fish, we saw that the deer had yet to cross through. On our way back from fishing, late in the morning, the tracks were loud and clear in the sand. Now we knew that he was coming through in the early morning rather than in the middle of the night. Which was good.

We cleaned our fish and froze the fillets when we got back to Groters's place. Then, in the afternoon, my old man and I drove back to Teapot Trail. We followed the deer tracks into the woods, being careful not to walk on the trail directly. Instead we paralleled it, so we didn't stink it up with human odor. We kept our talking to a whisper and were careful not to touch anything that wasn't necessary. We went about two hundred yards into the woods. Then we started looking for an ambush tree that sat within easy bow range of the trail. We wanted it to be in a place where the topography and undergrowth would offer some added encouragement for the deer to stay on the path and not wander willy-nilly through the woods. You'll know what I'm talking about if you ever follow a game trail into a meadow; often the trail will widen and lose its definition in the open and then funnel back down before it enters the woods again.

We found a tree that stood about fifteen yards off the trail in a downwind position. I screwed three L-shaped steps into the trunk of the tree, the third about chest high. Then I stood on the first step and held the third step with one hand while I screwed in the fourth. When I'd done about ten steps I was about sixteen feet up in the tree. I secured myself to the tree by fastening a safety belt that we'd removed from a car around my waist and the tree's trunk. I had a rope tied to my belt loop, and I used it to hoist up a chain, a chain binder, and a mounting bracket. After joining the bracket to the tree, I hoisted up a carpeted plywood platform that mounted to the bracket with a pair of bolts and wing nuts. That was to stand on. For a seat, I fastened above it a smaller metal platform that my old man had fabricated from a roadside speed limit sign that he'd pulled out of the ground somewhere. You could still see a portion of the numeral 35 on the upper side. The downward-facing side was painted a mottled green and brown for camouflage. Once my stand was up, we went deeper into the woods and hung my father's stand at the intersection of two well-used deer trails.

There was only one full day left before bow season opened, so we spent the next morning moving our stuff out of Groters's place and getting our camp pitched out in the woods along Teapot Trail. We took it easy that night and didn't stir around too much. Both of our tree stands were within a mile of camp, and my dad said it was important not to raise a lot of ruckus. We wanted to "give the place a rest," he said. We went to bed on army cots positioned against the walls of the tent.

Loud snorers are usually the first to fall asleep, and my old man was no exception. He snored loud and hard, as though he were exorcising some demon from his body. Now I wonder if that's not a bad explanation for what was going on inside of him. During the war, when he left Morocco, he was shipped out on a straw-lined railcar that started him on a circuitous land and sea route toward the Italian peninsula. On January 22, 1944, he took part in Operation Shingle.* The landing at the Anzio beachhead went smoothly compared to the Allied landings at Normandy that coming summer, but breaking away from the coast was difficult. The army was bogged down there for months. During that time my dad worked as a forward observer. He'd sneak out ahead of the front lines and climb up to a high piece of ground where he could sit with binoculars and search for the enemy. He looked for amassed troops, mortar positions, sometimes just a distant flash of sunlight on what looked to be the windshield of a vehicle. Then he'd radio coordinates back to the artillery positions, as estimated from a compass and a map. At first the artillery guys would launch white phosphorous rounds, which erupted with a highly visible plume of smoke. The location of the plume allowed him to fine-tune his coordinates. Once the phosphorous bombs were hitting on target, they'd cut loose with live rounds.

Those early months of combat had surreal elements. For one thing, my dad never met or saw the men who launched the bombs. The munitions usually came from ships in the Mediterranean, and they might as well have been dropped by God. At their closest, the Germans were usually thousands of yards away. If he considered them at all, it was only to remember that they'd gladly kill him if they had the chance. But his sense of removal dissolved with time. Once, he

*This is the battle where Pink Floyd bassist and songwriter Roger Waters's father, Eric Fletcher Waters, was killed. The man's death, and its effect on his son, is alluded to throughout Pink Floyd's The Wall, which is a great rock album for anyone who spends a lot of time pondering their old man.

spent the night out ahead of the front lines in the remnants of a building that had been bombed to rubble. In the middle of the night he
heard drunken singing. It was quiet and distant at first but got pro-
gressively louder as the source drew near. To his horror, he realized
that there were three voices and they were singing in German. He
couldn't fathom what they were doing, other than that they'd gotten
horribly lost without even knowing it. As they passed on the road in
front of his building he pulled a pin on a grenade and tossed it at their
feet.

Another story he told many times involved another bombed-out
building, this one at the crest of a prominent hill. He and his partner
had decided to set up an observation post inside. The only way in was
through a small window. He climbed through carrying a radio on his
back, a set of binoculars around his neck, and a Thompson subma-
chine gun in his hand. He described this action vividly to me, the way
he sat on the sill of the window before nudging himself forward and
dropping to the ground. Then, as soon as his boots hit, he smelled the
fresh and unmistakable odor of German cigarettes. Scattered all
around the basement were cigarette butts and discarded tins of food,
some of them so fresh that the juices hadn't dried. On the floor of the
building was a German soldier, still alive and staring at him with fear
and wonder. My dad figured him to be fourteen. The soldier's arm
was hanging on by threads of skin. The bone was shattered and jagged
and visible, and my dad guessed that he might have been hit by a
strafing round.

My dad eventually quit talking to people. Instead, he opted to
stare at the sky whenever he had a free moment. Alarmed, an officer
removed him from the lines and sent him to a field hospital. My dad
was seated in front of a doctor, but he didn't want to talk to him. The
doctor injected my dad with what he believes must have been some
sort of truth serum—possibly pentobarbital. The doctor asked,

"Where did you drop your rifle?" My dad said, "I didn't drop my rifle." The doctor waited a few moments and then repeated himself: "Where'd you drop your rifle?" The next thing my dad knew, it was hours later and he was sobbing in the doctor's lap.

He began hunting for big game when he got home. First he hunted with other veterans, men who had shared his experiences. Men like Groters, who had spent time in the service, became his confidants. Later he hunted with the first crop of three boys that he had with his first wife—my half brothers. By the time I was born, the youngest of those boys, Jimmy, a service member in the navy, had been killed in a motorcycle crash. The middle boy, Tony, had once lived in a tepee and fed himself and his wife on poached deer and porcupines that he killed with a bow. The oldest, Frank, was a game warden. My father didn't talk to any of them very often when I was a kid; he'd put his attentions to his new family. While he may have vowed to do some things differently on his second go-around as a father, he did not abandon the notion that his kids ought to be hunters.

Early in the morning, after the alarm woke us, my dad fried a batch of egg-in-the-holes in a skillet over a Coleman two-burner stove. He'd swapped the white gas fittings out for propane burners so that he could run the stove and the lamp through a Siamese connector fitted to a five-pound tank. The appliances hissed with a sound that, whenever I hear it today, still reminds me of camping with my old man. We ate standing. When we were done, we walked in the dark down Teapot Trail until we were close to our destination. Then the old man clicked on a disposable flashlight in order to look for the piece of surveyor's tape that we'd tied to a limb to mark our route into the woods.

At the base of my tree I pulled a twenty-five-foot length of parachute cord from my pack. My dad watched me tie one end of the cord to the limb of my bow and the other end to my belt loop. I started up the tree. Fear set in when I reached the last peg, because then I had to commit my weight to the stand and pull myself up. For some reason the stand always seemed like a tenuous structure in the dark. I grabbed the platform with all my strength and jumped upward a bit, so that my belly hit the platform's front edge. I then fell forward, so that the bulk of my body's weight came to rest on the platform. From there I could hug the tree and stand up. My dad waited as I pulled my bow up behind me and hung it on a limb I had sawed off. He took this as a sign that I was okay and then disappeared into the dark. I removed an arrow from my quiver and nocked it to the bow's string. Soon the noise of his boots on the dry leaves faded and he was gone.

Years earlier, I had begun sitting with my two brothers in tree stands that my dad placed above his own stand, so we could learn to hold still and be quiet despite the discomfort of being cold and having our body parts go numb from sitting for hours on end without moving. Then my brother Matt turned twelve when I was nine, and I started sitting with him in his tree stand. As a game we'd divide the woods in half, so that we were each responsible for watching a 180-degree swath of the forest, in order to see who could spot a deer first. Then Danny turned twelve the next year and I switched to his stand. I remember being up in a tree with Danny while he tried to convince me that it was unwise for me to swing my legs in an effort to mimic the way that the tree limbs were blowing in the breeze.

Now, at twelve years of age, I was all alone in a tree stand for the first time. Part of me took solace in being up in the tree, because at least I was safe from deer. My fear of deer was something I'd always been embarrassed about and had never admitted to anyone. It came from an experience that I'd had a couple of years earlier when I was sitting against a tree while hunting for squirrels. All of a sudden a three-by-three whitetail buck came walking right toward me through the woods. At first he didn't seem to notice I was there, so I grabbed a stick and snapped it in order to notify him. This got his attention, but in the wrong way. He started coming right at me, the way a dog will cross a yard in order to meet a stranger at the gate. I then recalled my dad coming home from a deer hunt once with his hand bandaged and full of sutures; he had been hunting from the ground and had hit a buck with his bow. The deer had charged him, knocking him down and causing him to slice himself open with his own arrowhead. That scene flashed through my mind, and I attempted to yell at this buck in a menacing way. I only managed a shriek. The deer stopped dead still, then blew a warning call and bounded off.

While I was at least safe from deer up in my tree, there were still bears to be afraid of. I had vivid memories of my dad getting a phone call late one night because his buddy was in the hospital after getting mauled by a black bear. This friend had been hunting from a tree stand when the sow had come along with two cubs. The bear must have caught the smell of danger because suddenly she chased her cubs up a tree toward safety. They picked the tree my dad's buddy was in, and then let out some excited yelps and hisses as the cubs passed him by. Before he could even think, the sow was up the tree and mauling him. She got through his boots and mauled his feet, ankles, and calves. All the while, he tried to repel her with an arrow. She didn't quit gnawing him until the cubs passed him by on their way down.

I couldn't think of the bear mauling that guy's legs without thinking of a bear rug that hung in our house when I was younger. It was from a black bear that my dad had killed in Ontario. He was hunting in the spring, right when the suckers were swimming out of the larger lakes to spawn in the rivers. Black bears knew about this source of food and my dad exploited their interest by hanging gunnysacks full of the fish along their trails. Then he built a ground blind with a frame of limbs covered by overlapped pine boughs. This particular bear was so thin from its winter hibernation that my dad could see its ribs spread apart when it reached out to tear open the bag of fish. He pulled back his recurve bow and placed an arrow between two of the ribs. The bear tore off into the trees, but it didn't make it far. My dad described the sensation of listening to the bear drown on its own blood. He said it gurgled and then bellowed like a wounded man as it died. He said the hair on the back of his neck stood up when he heard the noise. To demonstrate this part of the story, he would reach over and grab the hair at the back of my neck and pull it, as though the action would initiate the same level of fear in me. The only other time he mentioned this sensation was when he described jumping into a foxhole and coming face-to-face with a German soldier so decayed he had fly larvae coming out of his nasal passages. If the stories of the bear and the dead German had any other commonality, it was to illuminate the levels of brutality and tolerance that are sometimes required of men.

To sit in a tree and watch the coming of dawn is a strange thing. As soon as you can see the ground with any detail it seems that you're twice as high as you thought you were. Tree stumps go through brief periods when they look like people. The root wads of overturned trees look like bears. You can't tell whether the trail you're sitting along passes through a large meadow you should have noticed earlier or just a slight opening in the trees that you wouldn't have noticed earlier. But as the light comes up enough to make out the individual leaves on the ground, you realize that you're only as high as you thought you were. The stumps go back to being stumps, the root wads back to root wads. The trail begins to look like how you remembered it.

But then, after a while, the trail I was sitting above did not look at all how I remembered it. The buck was coming down it, moving with

an almost catlike sense of purpose. It was just like my father predicted, almost as if he had summoned the deer and sent it to me. In
the instant that I registered the animal's presence, I also registered the
idea that it would be beneath me within seconds. This realization was
outside the experiences that I'd had while sitting in a tree stand with
my dad or my brothers. Usually, we'd see deer coming along the edge
of a field far away, or coming from way back in the woods. There'd be
plenty of time to get accustomed to its presence. The initial adrenaline rush from seeing the animal would fade a little before you were
hit by the second adrenaline rush of having the animal come close.
But this deer was compressing that experience into a single moment,
stacking the rushes into a precarious heap. The pores on my skin
rushed open in a wave of heat, the way they do when you're in a sweat
lodge at the moment they pour the cold water over the hot rocks. My
knees weakened and my hands shook as I reached for my bow. The
three middle fingers on my left hand were protected by a split leather
tab, and I wrapped them around the bow's string—two fingers below
the nocked arrow, one above it.

At this point I could see the deer's shoulder from a lateral perspective. The moment that the deer's head passed behind a tree, I'd
pull back my bow and sink the arrow into the rear crease of the shoulder's muscle. At the time there were two competing thoughts in my
mind, one for each of the possible outcomes. The first was the thought
of killing the buck. I imagined the purity of the pride that my father
would feel; I imagined the glory of returning home with my first deer
and then going to school and bragging about it; I imagined us ribbing
Groters about how even a twelve-year-old could kill a deer cleanly
with a bow if he knew what he was doing.

The second was the thought of wounding the buck. I'd seen this
happen a few times already, and it was awful. One night, years earlier,
my dad had hit a deer with his bow and he took me and my brothers

out after dark to track it. All we could find were little pin drops of blood on the yellowish maple leaves of the forest floor. Some of the drops were purplish from bile, which meant a gut-shot deer that would be tough to find even though it would almost surely die within a few days. By midnight I was too tired and couldn't keep up, so my dad left Danny with me and told us to wait in the bottom of a ravine. He gave us one lantern and took Matt and the other lantern to push ahead. Our lantern ran out of gas and we had to wait in the cold dark. Around 1 A.M. our dad came back, having lost the deer's trail up ahead. He looked sick with self-disgust.*

As this deer rounded the tree, I was met with a third scenario that I could never have imagined. The strength in my arms had vanished, and I simply could not pull the bow back. I tugged and tugged, but the string wouldn't budge. The deer passed me by, never knowing I was there. Then, when the opportunity for a shot had passed, the string pulled back in my hands as easily as if I were practicing. I pointed the arrow in the direction of the deer, without really thinking about where it would go, and let the arrow fly.

It hit the ground beneath the buck, almost equidistant between the front and rear legs.

The deer ran off and then the forest grew quiet again. I climbed down and got my arrow, then climbed back up and cleaned the dirt off. I cleaned it so well that you'd never know I'd shot it. I could lie about this, I figured. I'd lied before. One time, when I was ice fishing, a guy had given me a huge northern pike because he didn't like how

---

*That night, driving home at around 2 A.M., my dad hit a yearling deer that jumped out in front of the truck, a Jeep Grand Cherokee. He picked it up and threw it into the back. Moments later, Matt and Danny were yelling and screaming from the backseat that the deer was alive. It was actually standing up in the rear of the Jeep. My dad slammed on the brakes, hauled the deer back out of the Jeep, cut its throat, let it bleed out, and then he threw it back in. The remainder of the eight-mile drive was uneventful.

bony their fillets were. I told him that I wished I'd caught that pike myself. The guy told me to stand off a ways, and then he tossed me the fish. "There," he said. "You caught it." That night, I showed my neighbor the fish and told him I'd caught it. I felt awful for days.

My dad came to get me a couple of hours after I missed the deer. I told him nothing happened, and we walked out together toward Teapot Trail. But as we got close to camp, I decided to come clean about the morning. I told him about being scared. About panicking when the deer came. About cleaning off the arrow. He reached out and put his hand on the back of my neck and held it there, gently, as we walked along.

Tasting Notes: Heart

First-deer rituals come in many forms, and usually involve some kind of eating or drinking. The movie *Red Dawn* popularized the ritual of downing a cup of blood dredged from the deer's chest cavity. Others say you should bite out a hunk of raw heart. A friend of mine from Montana described being forced to eat a slice of raw liver topped with a sprig of sagebrush. In Scotland it's a ritual to smear the hunter's cheeks with the blood of his first deer. When I hunted there and killed a red deer, the guy I was hunting with smeared his hand with blood and reached toward my face. I explained that I'd killed many deer before. "Not in Scotland," he said, and then gave me a swipe on each side of my face.

We didn't have any particular ritual in my family, as my dad wasn't big on symbolic acts of bravado. But he was big on eating deer hearts, the fresher the better, and when the heart came from my own first deer the meal was treated with even more respect than usual.

I killed it with a lever-action Winchester rifle, a year before I was old enough to do it legally. (Back then, you had to be twelve to hunt deer with a bow and fourteen to hunt them with a gun.) It was late in the morning, and we were doing something called a drive. Basically, a bunch of "pushers" head into an area where deer are known to bed during the day, and a "stander" positions himself where he thinks the deer will pass through as they run out. In this case, the bedding area was a deep ravine with a brushy creek bed at the bottom. My two brothers and a buddy of ours were the pushers who had to go down there and bust the deer out. I was the stander, and it was my job to hide on a hemlock-covered ridgeline that angled down into the ravine and provided a good vantage point to see what was going on below.

I saw the deer coming from way off. I expected it to pass below me as it followed the creek, but instead it broke away from the bottom and turned right up my ridgeline. It kept coming and coming, closer and closer. It didn't even know I was there until it was so close that we could have conversed in whispers. It then stopped behind a bent-over tree. All I could see was its head and a bit of its throat. I aimed for the throat but hit the jaw. The deer fell hard and then scrambled down the side of the ridge in a somersaulting flurry of legs. I was right there behind it when it reached the bottom of the ravine. I kept expecting it to die, but suddenly it regained its feet and started to make some progress. I was carrying a Green River beaver skinning knife on my belt like the mountain men did. I pulled the knife and threw an arm around the deer's neck and laid it down on its side like a cowboy in a roping competition. Then I put the tip of the knife into the deer's neck and sliced its jugular. Only later, after my brother pointed it out to me, did I realize that I could have just shot the thing a second time.

I used that same knife to gut the deer, which weighed damn near what I did. When I was done I dug through the entrails to find the sac—it's

Me with my first deer.

called a pericardium—that holds the heart. I could feel the warm firmness of the heart inside, about the size of a man's fist. When I sliced through the sac the heart slid out into my hand as though something were being born rather than killed. It wasn't until later that I would read about how some indigenous hunters fed the hearts of their quarry to their young children, so that the children would inherit the strengths and attributes of the animals they relied on. But I did know I was holding the core of a creature, the essence of its life, and that its life was far bigger and more meaningful than any squirrel's. It was impossible not to see just how serious the business of killing was.

I took off my blaze orange vest and wrapped the heart in it and put that into my day pack. My brothers then helped me drag the deer up out of the ravine and across a bunch of farm fields and through some windrows to where we'd parked that morning. At home my dad showed me how to take a thin-bladed fillet knife and carve out what are known as the great veins at the head of the heart. This left the heart looking deflated and a little hollowed out. I then started slicing the heart crosswise into slices about three-eighths of an inch thick, beginning at the narrow, pointy end. At first the slices were round and solid, like if you sliced a tree limb. But as I got deeper into the heart I began to hit the open pockets of the ventricles. These pockets started out small, just big enough for a pinky to fit through, but deeper into the heart they were so big that the slices looked as hollow as crosscut slices of a bell pepper.

My dad often deep-fried game in an electric fryer with a basket, but on this day we put a pan on the stove and filled it with a quarter-inch of oil. While the oil heated we spilled out some flour on a dinner plate and then dredged each of those slices through it. They sizzled when they hit the pan, and the oil came bubbling up through the holes of the ventricles, and the edges of the slices curled away from the heat. We took them off when they were crispy on the outside, though not so crispy that the juices didn't still run with a little blood.

In general we weren't allowed to put catsup on deer meat. My dad said it ruined the flavor. But with heart he made an exception. The meat was a little rubbery but snapped like a good hot dog when I bit into it. The flavor was similar to liver, though it wasn't as strong. And there was something kind of metallic about it, too, but in a pleasing way. In all, it was a strong and identifiable flavor that I would grow to love, and that I would enjoy for many years to come. Yet it would never become something that I'd want to eat every day or even every week. Why not? It's kind of hard to say. It was too . . . *something*. Perhaps the best word is one that some Vietnamese used to describe a meal of dog meat that we were sharing. They called it a "hot" food. Not hot like temperature or spicy hot. But hot as in volatile, in that you could feel it burning into your soul.

||||||||||||||||||||||||||||||||||||||||||||||||||||||||||||||||||||||||||||||||||||||||||||||||||||||||||||||||||

CHAPTER FIVE

The Otter

★

I WAS IN MY canoe, scouting for muskrat and beaver sign in a swampy backwater that drained through a narrow channel into a creek about six miles from my house. As I paddled along, I heard what sounded almost like a dog splashing and barking behind a curtain of cattails. I nosed the canoe ahead and there was a river otter, the first I ever saw in my life. It was eating a bluegill with so much vigor that I could hear the fish's bones crunching from forty yards out. It hissed at me when it noticed me, the sound coming through a mouthful of fish as though the animal were playing a harmonica. Then it crunched the rest of the bluegill down, tail last, and slipped beneath the water's surface so smoothly that it could have been a chunk of black ice dissolving instantaneously into the water. I followed the otter's wake as it swam toward the mouth of the marsh. It passed through the body-wide channel with a splash and disappeared into the creek, heading downstream.

It had been almost eight years since my brothers and I caught our first muskrats on North Lake. Matt and Danny had stayed in the trapping business only a few years, calling it quits when the 1987 stock market crash put an end to the decade-long fur boom. After that it got harder and harder to sell fur, though I remained committed to the trapper's way of life. I continued to plug along under the delusional conviction that fur prices would suddenly and inexplicably come bouncing back—regardless of the fact that America's appetite for fur had begun to vanish in ways that could not be explained strictly through economics. In many parts of the country, it had become a moral issue as well. Still, I was positive that this coming fall was going to be my best season yet; I planned to catch enough fur to demonstrate to myself and others that trapping was a legitimate way to make a living and not just some anachronistic daydreamer's pastime. To do that would take luck, and in some weird way it seemed as though the otter was symbolic of luck's arrival.

After all, the animals had been nearly eradicated from this region through habitat destruction from logging, overharvest by trappers, and wanton slaughter by fishermen who resented the competition over a limited resource. In recent decades, though, the animals had been making a miraculous comeback and were slowly spreading their way southward into areas that hadn't seen otters in many years. Now, apparently, they'd expanded their range into my own territory. As someone who loved wilderness and water, I could hardly help but admire this creature that combined those two elements with such perfect grace. Even though the animals were still off-limits to trappers in this area, I felt as though the otter's presence on my trapline could help bring back the frontier that I had been born too late to experience. Maybe, along with that, it had brought back the ability for a man to make his living in the wilderness.

When I graduated from high school, earlier that summer, I was relieved that school would no longer interfere with my time in the woods. The only problem was that my old man had a rule that you couldn't live at his house unless you were actively in school and getting good grades. So I was faced with the annoyance of having to move out unless I enrolled in college. And since moving out took a lot of time and a good job, I opted for school. I signed up at a local community college that was only twenty minutes from my home. Friends from high school jokingly referred to it as the thirteenth grade. There I could take a semester's worth of classes for six hundred dollars, which was way cheaper than paying my own rent. I went through the course catalog and picked out a bunch of night classes that included an aerobics course. This schedule had me in class only Monday through Thursday, 6 P.M. to 9 P.M. Life was looking good.

I busted my ass all summer. I had a job six nights a week, from midnight to 3 A.M., cleaning a green bean processing plant with high-pressure hoses. We used duct tape to seal the ankles and sleeves of our rain gear to keep out some of the water. I'd come home and sleep until mid-morning, and then I'd go into the woods to cut firewood. I sold green firewood for sixty-five dollars a cord, or 128 cubic feet. I saved as much wood as I could for later, because a cord of dry wood fetched ninety dollars in January.*

All along, my plan was to save up enough money through the summer to finance my entire four-month trapping season. That way I'd be able to stretch and dry all my pelts and hold them until late January, when I'd sell them at the annual Michigan Trappers Association fur auction in Ravenna. The auction drew in fur buyers from around the Midwest and Canada, and the competitive bidding process usually jacked the prices up significantly from what you'd get by making a private visit to one of these fur buyers' homes.

---

*Selling firewood could be great money or it could really suck, depending on the circumstances. A cord of wood is 128 cubic feet and can weigh anywhere from 3,000 to 5,000 pounds. I had a rack for my 1984 Chevy three-quarter-ton 4x4 pickup that could accommodate such a load, and I'd beefed up the leaf springs to keep the truck's bed from scraping the rear axle. Still, with a full load the truck was almost impossible to handle because the front tires seemed to float off the ground and the steering wheel had only a touch of resistance when you turned it.

But despite my best efforts, I just couldn't put away the kind of money that I needed. All summer I was faced with the expenses of empty gas tanks, truck breakdowns, and chain saw repairs. Plus, there were a lot of costs associated with the coming trapping season. I needed to buy new traps, update old equipment, get a new canoe, and tune my vehicle for the rigors of off-road driving. That fall, after paying college tuition and buying books, I went into the October 15 fox and coyote opener with only a few hundred dollars saved up.

The season got off to a slow start. Two weeks of hard trapping yielded only seven red foxes, two gray foxes, two coyotes, and a dozen or so raccoons. By the time mink and muskrat season opened, on Sunday, November 1, I'd already had to take a small loan from my dad to keep me afloat. I set well over sixty traps that day, working from way before sunrise to way after sunset. The next day I had what I knew would be the best haul of the season: twenty-seven muskrats, six raccoons, and a mink. Before driving to school, I dropped by my house and grabbed my stretched fox and coyote pelts and put them on the front seat of my truck. That night I paid a visit to an area fur buyer named Abe. This guy bought a lot of raw, unfinished pelts and made some of his money on the markup that he'd get by fleshing and stretching them. He was a touch overweight, and wore old sweatshirts with the sleeves cut off at the wrists. His hair was pretty long for an old man and he combed it straight back. In the winter, he heated his workshop with gobs of raccoon fat that he'd scrape off the hides and toss into a barrel stove to burn.

My dad never trusted Abe because of something that had happened one time when I'd killed a mink with a rifle when I was hunting deer. I'd been watching a chipmunk scurrying in and out of the labyrinth of exposed roots created by a beech tree that had tipped over. All of a sudden, the mink ran over and chased the chipmunk

Me with a load of fur after a long day of trapping. About thirty muskrats on the tailgate, a pair of raccoons in hand.

into a hole. The chipmunk must have given it the slip, though, because the mink came back up empty-mouthed and started scouring the root structure with a vengeance. When the animal saw me, it looked right at me and hissed like a snake. Mink were worth forty dollars then, so I took aim. The bullet took off its head and removed an inch-wide strip of fur that ran about six inches down the mink's back. My dad and I spent over an hour carefully skinning what was left of the mink and getting it tacked out nicely on a wooden stretcher. My father came away from the project with the attitude that the partial animal should be worth more than a regular mink, just because of the work he put into it. Abe disagreed. The mink was missing a significant portion of the most valuable part of its fur, he explained. The center strip from the mink's back goes into the nicest coats. He offered only twenty dollars. I now realize that Abe was actually being quite generous, but my father never forgave the slight. He contended that Abe's crookedness was linked to his ethnicity—which was okay for my dad to say, because he was Italian, too—and so I maintained my own cautious approach in my business dealings with Abe.

However cautious I was, nothing could have prepared me for Abe's offer. When he got done looking at my pelts, he told me that the best he could do was $350 for the entire haul. Of course, I had known that fur prices were down, but I didn't realize they were *that* down. Back in 1984, when I'd started trapping, that haul of furs would have been worth thousands of dollars. Now here I was, and the furs didn't even have enough value to keep me flush with cash for another week. What's more, it didn't come close to covering the investments I'd made in equipment. Abe must have registered my desperation, because he pulled out a plastic package containing coils of cable that I immediately recognized as snares.

Even though the technology of a snare is ancient and extremely simple—an animal walks through a loop and the loop closes around its body and holds it—it remains one of the most efficient tools for catching furbearing animals today. The problem with snares, at least in the eyes of their critics, is that this efficacy is somewhat indiscriminate. While a trapper sets his snares to catch his targeted species around the neck, it's easy for larger species such as deer (or livestock) to get their feet caught up in snares. What's more, should the trapper forget where he set them or neglect to collect them, snares are much more likely than regular traps to stay in working order for a long period of time and through all kinds of bad weather. Even a snare that's been knocked over and covered in snow can still snag a deer's hoof or the paw of someone's pet dog. And since a snare doesn't kill such large animals outright, it's possible for them to suffer a long time before they either die from exhaustion or starvation or a predator gets hold of them. And while all of these problems can be alleviated and even eliminated through caution and diligence on the part of those using snares, the law doesn't always trust people to do what's right. So snares are heavily regulated in much of the country and outright prohibited in the rest—including the state that I happened to be in.

Still, Abe told me to go ahead and try them out. "If you don't like 'em, give the ones you don't use back. If you do like 'em, you can pay me in fur on your next visit." He set them down on his workbench and started to count out my money. When he was done, I grabbed the cash and left with the snares in my pocket.

The snares were on my mind more or less constantly over the next month. I kept them tucked between the springs and the foam on the underside of my pickup's bench seat, and I could almost hear them calling to me as I drove around. But I didn't actually pull them out until a week or so after Thanksgiving. By then the general deer season was over and the woods were quiet and empty of people, and the lakes and ponds were beginning to freeze up. I was setting muskrat traps along a stream, where the moving water would keep the ice off for another month or so. While taking breaks to warm my fingers, I studied the banks of the stream to see what sorts of tracks might have collected in the snow. In one place, where the stream made a sharp curve to the left, I noticed a single set of tracks that came down to the bank and crossed a snow-covered log that had fallen like a bridge across a smaller tributary stream. From a distance I could tell that they were made by a fox, because the animals tend to place their feet in a straight line when they walk. That is, if a fox took ten steps you'd be able to pull a string tight and lay it across nine of them.* I walked over to the tracks to have a more careful look. Not many people know this, but a fox will often use the same trail again and again in the snow without leaving more than one set of prints. Each time the animal passes through, it'll put its feet back into the holes that it used the

---

*Place a string along the trail of a domestic dog and you'll only hit four or five of its tracks. Coyotes walk straighter than a domestic dog, but not as straight as a fox.

last time. Examining the tracks, I could tell that was happening here. The bottom of the track was not just a clean imprint of a single paw; instead, it was an oval of packed snow made from several footfalls.

Normally I wouldn't have paid much attention to these tracks, because the weather conditions at that time of year—snow and fluctuating temperatures—make foothold traps very difficult to work with. During the day, whenever the air temperature rose up above freezing, the dirt or snow that I used to conceal my fox traps would become saturated with water. Then, at night, when the temperature dropped back down, the covering would freeze so hard that you couldn't trigger the trap with a hammer let alone with the delicate touch of a fox's paw.

But the snares I'd gotten were fairly indifferent to snow. I stood there for a while and thought about this, then walked all the way back to my truck and pulled a couple of the snares out from beneath the seat. I used my lineman's pliers to snip off a length of eight-gauge wire. I fastened that to the swivel end of the snare and then wrapped the remaining end around the base of a tree. I then cut a dead limb with my hatchet and jabbed it into the ground so that it stood up like a flagpole right next to the log. To this limb I attached a small tab of fourteen-gauge wire. After opening the loop of the snare into a circle with a nine-inch diameter, I used the tab of wire to support it in a position that was eight inches directly over the log. If the fox came back, his head would pass through the loop.

That's exactly what happened. When I came back two days later, the nicest fox that I'd caught all year was waiting for me. It had wrapped itself around the anchor tree like a tetherball, and it was stone dead and half frozen. The only thing that surprised me more than the fox's presence was my reaction to it. Normally, catching a fox gave me a rush of pride. They are known for their wiliness, and catching them was a validation of my woodsmanship. But seeing this fox in the snare bothered me in a deep way.

It wasn't as though I'd never broken a game law. One time, not long before this happened, my brother Matt and I sold forty gallons of smelt for forty dollars. That's illegal.* Another time, while hunting squirrels near the White River, I killed a salmon with a shotgun. That's also illegal. However, those were semi-spontaneous instances that seemed to pit my juvenile rationality against the letter of the law. When the guy offered to buy the smelt from us, we sold them under the justification that the smelt were already dead anyway, so what was the difference? Besides, we could have legally *given* the fish away, so what was wrong with taking a little gas money in exchange? As for the salmon, that fish had taken so many wrong turns on its upstream migratory journey that it was lolling around in a dead-end cattail marsh. Never in a hundred years would she find a mate or a suitable bed of gravel on which to deposit her eggs. Wasn't it just as good for the salmon to end up in my dad's fish smoker as it was to rot on the bottom of the marsh?

As much as I tried to use similar logic to justify the act of setting the snare, I really couldn't make it work. I knew it was wrong, plain and simple. Not only was it a premeditated and explicit violation of the game laws, it was a violation of the *spirit* of the game laws. Not only do hunters abide by regulations in order to even the playing field between us and our quarry, we abide by game laws in order to even the playing field between one another. By agreeing to operate under the same sets of rules and conditions, hunters divide available re- sources according to skill and determination rather than a free-for-all

*It is illegal for individuals to sell wild-caught fish and wild game. There are some exceptions with fish, but none with birds and animals. When you buy such things as deer or elk or pheasant in a restaurant, you are buying farm-raised captive animals.

system of lawless opportunism. To violate the pact is as much a sin against other hunters as it is a sin against nature.

I wish I could say that I considered all of this and then tossed the snares into Mosquito Creek, but I can't. Rather, the guilt that I felt served only to egg me on. One half of me despised the other half for feeling bad, and that first half wanted to attack the second half. I was like a guy who wishes he could punch a concrete wall without getting hurt, and so he does it over and over again until he develops the necessary level of tolerance. My version of wall punching was to begin setting snares just about anywhere that I felt like it, regardless of safety. I set them along game trails leading to road-killed deer that had obviously been visited by domestic dogs. I set them near popular hiking trails on national forest lands. I set them in the rows of pine tree plantations frequented by rabbit hunters and their beagles.

I recognized the outlaw nature of what I was doing, and I managed to draw the usual parallels between myself and my bygone heroes. Popular mythology aside, Daniel Boone was not just some prince of the wilderness out looking to rescue distressed settlers from savage Indians. He was a professional market hunter, through and through. He killed animals in order to sell their hides and meat. And like any enterprising businessman, he wanted to procure his product line in the cheapest, most efficient way possible. Often that meant breaking the law. The western lands that Boone regarded as free and open were anything but. Fearing that Euro-American intrusion onto Indian lands beyond the Appalachians would upset the tribes and disturb the lucrative fur trade, the British crown passed law after law meant to prevent colonial hunters such as Boone from operating there. To do so was a clear violation of the law. But many of Boone's western explorations occurred during the years leading up to and including the American Revolution, a time when there was a lot of animosity toward the British. The Americans resented their meddling, and to violate British rule was hardly considered a moral infraction. What's more, the violation of Indian claims to the land had long ago been established as the American way of doing business; Boone certainly did not toss and turn at night over the thought of screwing some Indians out of their livelihoods.

While Boone had the British crown to rebel against, I had PETA. People for the Ethical Treatment of Animals had come onto the scene in 1980 and had gained steady traction throughout the decade. While they've become something of a self-parody in recent times, they were a powerful force back then. They did an effective job of portraying trapping as a brutish and unnecessarily cruel throwback to man's darker and more exploitative past. They discussed trapping through a lexicon of suffering—"barbaric," "inhumane," "excruciating"—and they supplied a never-ending litany of images showing panic-stricken household pets and stoic wild animals gripped heartlessly in the jaws of traps. While I had seen things that would make PETA posters look like ads for Disney movies, I was deeply insulted by the message they were putting forth. As far as I could see, trappers had built this country and made it what it was, and now these softies were questioning the very foundation of our history.

Also, they were having a serious impact on the public perception of fur and, by extension, fur prices. A lot of people didn't give a hoot what PETA said, obviously, but the organization's activities meant that any discussion of fur products would inevitably turn to a discussion about red paint getting thrown on fur garments. And while economic realities were certainly the primary source of the global fur market collapse—after all, Russian, Italian, and Chinese women had yet to even hear of PETA—I had a hard time focusing my anger in that direction. Instead I regarded PETA as an evil and un-American force that was assaulting me in both personal and financial ways.

My paranoia only increased one day when a game warden pulled in behind me while I was parked where a gas pipeline intersected Cedar Creek in Manistee National Forest. My first impulse was to wonder how he knew I was there. Had he followed me in from the main road? But then it occurred to me that the answer was as simple as the fresh snow on the ground. He saw a set of tracks going into the woods and none coming back out, and did the math.

I watched in my side-view mirror as he pulled up to my tailgate in such a way that I was prevented from backing out. Reflexively, I grabbed the snow camo jacket off the seat next to me and tossed it over the snares. I had been eating a pocketful of jerky and warming my toes in the truck's heater when the warden pulled up, so I stepped out of the truck and kept right on chewing in order to convey a sense of nonchalance and innocence. The warden stepped from his own truck with his hand rested casually on his sidearm, in a manner suggesting that he'd been trained to do it that way. He took a couple of steps toward me and jumped right into the matter at hand: "How's trapping?" he asked.

"Going all right. Prices are down bad, you know."

"Mind if I have a look in the back of your truck?" he asked.

"Go ahead."

I opened up the gate on the topper. Inside, I had my traps and equipment organized in wooden crates that were lined with straw and pine boughs in order to ward off unnatural odors. I never handled my traps with bare hands, because animals would smell my scent and avoid them, but that didn't stop the warden from reaching in bare-handed to check my traps for the mandatory identification tags. Usually, a warden might just check one or two traps to make sure you're in compliance, but this guy went through every single trap I had with me—probably about four dozen. Then he started snooping around in some of the other crates. I knew from his thoroughness that he was trying to make some kind of a point or other. He didn't keep me wondering for long.

"You been setting any snares?" he asked.

I looked him right in the eye. "No, sir."

"You know anyone who's been setting them?"

"No, sir."

With that he climbed back into his truck and drove off.

I was still stinging from that encounter a few days later when I headed down into the swamp where I'd seen the river otter earlier that summer. My goal was to make some under-ice sets for muskrats. It was the perfect time of year for that, because there was plenty of ice. You could walk into swampy areas that were otherwise difficult to reach without a boat. Also, the ice made it easy to find animals. Muskrats exhale as they swim underwater, and the ice collects the bubbles in a telltale line that marks perfectly their line of travel. In a place where a lot of animals are traveling through, the bubbles collect so densely that it looks like a solid white line. You can find these even under a layer of snow, just by sweeping likely areas clean with a broom. Then all you do is chop through the ice with an ax and position a trap in the path.

I made a few sets near some muskrat lodges in the back of the marsh, and eventually I worked my way out toward where the swamp drained through the narrow channel into the creek. The ice ended at the mouth of the channel, and the stream flowed by as open water. On the lip of ice at the creek's edge I could see some slimy black pellets that were about the size of walnuts. I inched forward on the thin ice to have a better look. I'd read that otters will regurgitate the bones and scales of their prey, and that seemed to be what I was looking at on the ice. The greasy black pellets were full of crayfish shells and fish scales and bones. The otter was probably still in the area and was likely using the channel to access its fishing grounds beneath the ice of the swamp. He was climbing up here to rest and, presumably, to catch his breath before diving beneath the ice to fish.

I sat there for a long time thinking about what I should do. I thought about the otter, how happy I'd been to see it that summer. I thought of how it had promised me a good year. But I also thought about how I could probably sell that thing for a lot of money. Otters were a rarity in this area. If I didn't get a good offer from a fur buyer, I knew that I'd make decent money by selling it to a taxidermist who would mount it and then sell it as a decoration. The risks were pretty small, really. You were allowed to catch one otter per year just ten miles north of where I was. All I had to do was lie about where this happened.

Today it's difficult for me to explain all of this in a way that makes sense, perhaps because there's no good explanation. All I can really say is what I did, which is pull a trap from my pack and use it to block the entrance to the channel. I then poked a few sticks in the mud to guide the animal where I wanted it to go. I argued to myself that I'd probably just catch a muskrat. But I knew that the trap I was setting, a 220 Conibear, was better for catching an otter. And that's just what happened. When I came back, two days later, the otter that had once brought me so much happiness was dead in the trap. I made about fifty bucks so that some lady that I'd never meet in a country that I'd probably never visit could have a nice coat.

Thinking back on that now, I'm reminded of an acquaintance who loves to give the testimony about when he became a born-again Christian. In his telling, he keeps his narrative very tightly focused on his pre-Christian exploits. There were rough-and-tumble bar fights, drugs, women, good times, crazy music, fast motorcycles, and plenty of long hair blowing in the breeze. Eventually, of course, the story becomes true to its own purpose and he gets around to the logical conclusion of finding God and settling down. But every time he tells this story, you can see him getting carried away all over again by the fun and excitement of those days, and by how much he loves his former self.

I admit that there's an element of that at play here, in that I loved my days as a trapper. I learned and saw many things. I chased a dream that I believed in. I sacrificed for something that was elusive and difficult. But on the day that I killed the otter, I'd accomplished something else, as well: I'd become an asshole.

‖‖

Tasting Notes: Jerky

When I was a little kid, my old man built a plywood box with pine trim that was about the size of a dishwasher. He mounted the box on casters, capped the front with a bottom-hinged door, and fitted the inside walls with enough runners to support eight sliding shelves made of wire mesh. He cut a rectangular hole into the top of the door and covered it with an adjustable vent cover. He cut a circular hole in the lower back wall of the box, and rigged into that hole a dish-dryer motor from an old broken-down dishwasher. The whole thing cost not even a dollar, and you could dry about a half deer's worth of jerky at a time in there.

If you consider dried meat to be a recipe, then it's likely the first one that we as humans ever came up with. You can imagine it happening: Some guy long ago was picking shreds of sun-dried meat from a weeks-old lion kill and he got to thinking. The next time he came across a fresh carcass, he hung strips of the meat on bushes and let them dry in the wind and sun. The next day, when he had to move on, he was able to carry the remainder of the meat with him rather than leaving it for the scavengers and maggots. It probably wasn't too long before we learned that a little salt rubbed into the meat made it even more resistant to bacterial growth during the drying process. Our taste buds conformed to the necessity of salt and began to crave it. Voilà! The American hunter's favorite treat was born, though it was born far from America.

That you see commercially produced jerky hanging from display racks in gas stations is no accident, at least not in a historic sense. Jerky is, and was, traveling food. In a way, we can thank it for the fact that our ancestors were able to spread out around the globe. As early humans passed into new territories, traveling from island to island and across deserts, they were in constant danger of entering territory where they couldn't find anything to eat. The best way to mitigate risk would have been to carry food with them, and the best food for that purpose was jerky. It was what you grabbed when you were on the road. Historical accounts are full of anecdotes about war parties of young Native American men headed out to hunt and kill other Native Americans in hostile terrain with nothing besides a few bags of dried meat to sustain them. Some of the most famous Euro-American buffalo hunters—the same men who helped put the Indians out of business by eradicating their food source—rode into new country with nothing for food besides a sack of salt tied to their saddle horn. They were mobile and highly lethal, powered by jerky. There are photos that capture the scene: filthy, scruffy-looking white hide hunters in a camp where the ground is covered in pegged-out buffalo hides and the surrounding trees are hung with strips of jerky like Christmas ornaments. Not only did the meat help them move about without fear of going hungry, but it helped them stay put without fear as well. When hunters were preparing for a long, cold winter in camp, the most important thing to do was put up a generous supply of jerky. In December 1860, a force of Texas Rangers and American cavalry ransacked a Comanche camp that contained more than seven and a half tons of dried meat. At the time, there were only about fifteen people in the camp.

Of course, we don't eat jerky entirely out of necessity these days. You can kill a deer in October and then eat fresh-tasting meat for the next year thanks to freezers. But the original attributes that made it appealing still apply today. When I was running traplines, I'd cram a Ziploc full of jerky into my coat pocket in the morning. Sometimes, that would be all I'd eat for the entire day. The meat could stay in my pocket for weeks and it would taste pretty much the same no matter what happened to it. If it got wet, I'd set it over the heater vent on my dashboard to dry it back out. If it got dirty, I'd dust it off. After eating a handful, I'd usually have an unchewable wad of connective tissue rolling around in my mouth. Baseball players have mouthfuls of their trademark chewing tobacco; hunters have animal sinew.

Since my trapping days I've eaten many forms of jerky. I lived with a Blackfeet guy in Montana during graduate school and his family made jerky the old way, by hanging the meat on lines in the sun and letting it dry naturally. No salt or anything. He'd go home to his reservation over the weekend and come back with a stack of it. Meat like that has a weird sort of metallic taste, at least to me. I hunted with native Hawaiians who season their axis deer jerky in a teriyaki marinade and then dry it in screened boxes outside to keep the bugs off. That was some of the best I've eaten. Some of the worst I've eaten was collared peccary in Texas, sprinkled with salt and pepper and dried in the hot desert air. It tasted the way collared peccary smell, which isn't a compliment, though I respected the critter and ate all of it. Another time I spent a couple of weeks hunting with Makushi tribesmen in Guyana and they kept a constant supply of meat drying on racks over a fire. We ate dried black curassow and crestless curassow that we shot out of trees with bows. We ate large dried rodents called paca, which look like chipmunks that are about the size of medium dogs and which taste like superb pork. We ate dried fish, too, ranging from piranhas to peacock bass to electric eels. A few years ago I killed a buffalo with a flintlock muzzle-loader and dried the jerky on a handmade rack next to the Yellowstone River—something that surely happened thousands and thousands of times in the past but that doesn't happen much anymore.

My favorite way to make jerky is pretty tame by comparison. The finished product isn't much different from what you might see at your local gas station. First I'll pull a couple of mule deer shoulders from my freezer. I put them on the kitchen counter until they're thawed just enough to slice with a very sharp knife. I cut my strips going with the grain, usually an inch or two wide, five or six inches long, and about a quarter-inch thick. I'm not too picky about getting all the fat and sinews trimmed away, because I'm as interested in quantity as I am in quality. I've toyed around with many homemade concoctions and spice blends, but it's really hard to beat the commercially produced jerky seasonings that are sold at sporting goods stores. They come in little boxes with instructions, a bag of seasonings, and a bag of curing salts. Mix up the seasoning and cure, then sprinkle it on the meat according to the recommended dosage and let it set for a day or two. When I'm ready to dry it, I lay it out on squares of quarter-inch hardware cloth cut to fit the racks in my oven. I set the oven at its lowest setting. You want some air flow, so I put an empty beer can against the top of the door and crinkle the door closed against it.

At first the house fills with an odor that smells nothing like the jerky tastes, something like warm blood. My wife hates it, but she agrees that the end product makes it worthwhile. (If that smell gets too strong, your oven is too hot.) Once the odor begins to fade, I start checking the meat every half hour or so. Within a few hours of the start I'll be pulling the first pieces off. They're done when they feel as light as jerky. If you need more of an indicator than that, try breaking a piece. It should bend without snapping, and reveal fine little white lines along the fold. After it cools, I put it in gallon-sized Ziplocs. With a few of those bags in my backpack, I can leave home knowing that I'm ready for anything.

||||||||||||||||||||||||||||||||||||||||||||||||||||||||||||||||||||||||||||||||||||||||||||||||||||||||||||||||||||||

CHAPTER SIX

Communion

★

Mʏ sᴏɴ, Jɪᴍ, was born on May 9, 2010, and by the time he was a month old he was drinking two or three ounces of breast milk every two or three hours. What was surprising to me was that Katie produced milk even more prodigiously than he consumed it. Between feedings, she'd spend fifteen minutes pumping the excess milk with a little pump that resembled the device I use to purify creek water when I'm camping.

After pumping, she'd pour the milk into sealable plastic pouches about the size of a T-shirt pocket. She'd then label each pouch with the date, the quantity of milk in ounces, and the boy's name—James Rinella. Finally, she'd deposit the pouches according to date into master containers with sealed lids. These would go into the freezer. Every few days, she'd announce with pride that she'd put away enough milk to feed the boy through x period of time in case of some emergency that incapacitated her or her breasts—first it was a day, then five days, then two weeks.

Generally, my wife is not a food-oriented person. She does not enjoy cooking. As for our vegetable garden, she derives more pleasure from simply knowing it's there than she does from actually working in it. So I was surprised by the care and attention that she gave to the milk. I think she was surprised, too. One day, she was organizing the pouches of breast milk in the freezer and she turned to me and said, "I think I finally understand what it is with you and hunting. It's really satisfying to stock food away for someone you love. It's good knowing it's there, and that I did it, and that it was done right."

I wish that it hadn't taken Katie four years of us being together to finally understand "what it is with me and hunting." However, I can hardly criticize her lengthy delay in recognizing the inherent and inseparable connection between hunting and food. After all, it took me about twenty years to figure out the same thing. It happened in the fall of 1994, while I was hunting deer from a tree with a bow and arrow. The set of circumstances was remarkably similar to the first time I missed a buck, except for a few notable things: One, this buck was coming at me through the woods with more antler riding on its head; and two, I was sitting in a tree with a lot more responsibility hovering over mine.

In order to give that moment the attention it deserves, I should probably back up and explain the time period that preceded it. It's fair to say that at around that time my lifelong goal of becoming a professional trapper had crumbled into soul-sucking mayhem and I didn't know what to do with myself anymore. I needed to find a purer and more deliberate hunting life, and to do that I needed to go someplace that was fresh and new.

For guys from Michigan—or at least for those who love to hunt and fish—someplace fresh and new has always been the UP. That's Michigander lingo for the Upper Peninsula, the portion of the state lying north of the narrow strait formed where Lake Michigan feeds into Lake Huron. Michigan acquired it back in 1836 as a consolation prize after losing a bitter border dispute with Ohio over a chunk of land known as the Toledo Strip.* That area turned into . . . well, Toledo. Meanwhile, the UP proved largely resistant to development. Today, it's a kind of miniature Canada, but without the self-righteousness, progressive politics, or Draconian gun laws. In other words, it's possible to sit on the ice in the UP and watch a pack of wolves kill a moose while you fish for muskellunge, a collection of occurrences that you would certainly not experience in the woods where I grew up.

For us, the Mackinac Bridge was the equivalent of Daniel Boone's Cumberland Gap. It separated us from a mythic hunting ground, a place that oozed with adventure. A lot of my dad's friends would spend all their vacation time up there, living out of camper trailers while chasing fish and game. In the spring they'd bring home coolers full of walleye fillets and so many smelt they'd end up tilling them into their gardens as fertilizer. They'd come home in the fall with whitetail deer stacked in the back of their trucks like cordwood. It was an annual tradition of toll operators on the Mackinac Bridge to count how many deer headed south out of the UP on trucks and trailers. In 1994, the year I finally moved there, the total was 8,903. No one even bothered looking for deer headed in the opposite direction.

What kept these Trolls—that's UP lingo for people from below the bridge—from moving to the UP full-time was the lack of work and professional opportunity. To actually live there wouldn't have occurred to me if my brothers hadn't tried it first. In 1991, they both

---

*The Toledo Strip measured 468 square miles. Each state wanted it because they figured it would be a perfect location for a shipping canal connecting Lake Erie to Lake Michigan. Ultimately Ohio got the strip and Michigan accepted the nine-thousand-square-mile Upper Peninsula despite their characterization of the land as "a sterile region on the shores of Lake Superior destined by soil and climate to remain forever a wilderness." Then, thirty years later, my home state sat back and laughed when Ohio's canal was never built and the UP became the nation's leading supplier of iron ore and copper.

moved to the UP to pursue biology degrees at Lake Superior State
University in Sault Sainte Marie. Our dad, who'd dropped out of high
school and later earned a GED, described his two sons as having "ma-
jors in hunting and minors in fishing." His assessment wasn't far off.
They lived way the hell away from town, in a cabin along the St.
Maries River. In order to stretch their meager student loan incomes,
they motored their johnboat out from their house and landed it on
Neebish Island to hunt deer. They each killed a doe out there on public land with their bows, and then fed themselves on the meat for a
couple of months. Their venison diet was supplemented with fish and
ducks from the river and snowshoe hares from the cedar swamps that
stretched away from the river. Later, they would lose the security deposit on their cabin for getting blood all over the carpet.

Matt moved away from the UP after one semester, in order to attend his third college as an undergraduate.* The next fall Danny
moved into a cabin closer to town in order to save on gas money. He
was joined there by our friend from back home, Matt Drost. That
year, Danny and Drost each won the lottery drawing for a black bear
permit. They made bait piles in the cedar swamps using fish guts and
expired food that they scavenged from Dumpsters behind restaurants
in town. By mid-September, just a few weeks into the semester, they
were feeding themselves on a two-hundred-pound boar black bear
that Danny killed with his rifle. More deer followed. Then, after the
fall hunting season, Danny and Drost maintained their stash of wild
game by spearing whitefish and menominee through a hole that they
sawed into the ice of Lake Superior.

My introduction to this new form of subsistence lifestyle came
when I visited Danny the following year, in the late summer of 1993.

*If Matt seems like a fickle college attendee, consider this: He ended up getting a grad-
uate degree from the same school where he got his bachelor's degree, which isn't too
common. Then he spent four years at the same institution while getting a PhD.

Danny's first bear, from the UP.

I timed my visit to coincide with the pink salmon run.* The fish travel upstream out of Lake Huron to spawn in the large rapids formed where Lake Superior drops some twenty feet into the St. Maries River. The day I got there, Danny and I walked with our fishing rods to a dock not far from the Edison Sault dam. Giant freighters hauling coal

---

*The Sault Rapids had three actual fish runs and two rather mythical fish runs. The first of the actual runs every year was the steelhead run. (For a refresher on steelhead, see page 127 of this book.) They'd come up out of Lake Huron sometime in late May or early June, depending on weather, and then hang around until July. Then there'd be a lapse of activity until the pink salmon, which constituted another actual run, starting in late August or early September or thereabouts and petering out in October. Finally, the king salmon would come up in late September and hang around for a month or so. Atlantic salmon and a strain of steelhead known as Skamania represented the mythical fish runs, though both of these mythical fish populations have undergone significant developments in the ensuing years and interested parties would be wise to consult updated information sources on their current status. One final note: None of the fish I'm discussing here are actually native to the Great Lakes. They are all oceanic transplants. But that's a whole other story.

and iron ore slogged past in the river. The pink salmon came by in pulses, sometimes in scattered batches of four or five fish, sometimes in schools containing dozens of fish. Some of the schools were so dense with the two- to four-pound salmon that they looked like aqua-green submarines cruising beneath the river's surface.

Using spinning rods, we cast out lures and dragged them through the schools. The fish would usually clear out of the way of the lure, but when you got lucky, one of them would bust free from the school in order to slash at it. Whenever we hooked a salmon, the fish would zing out line and dive hard and fast toward deeper water. When it wore out, it would rise back up toward the surface and we'd scoop it up with a landing net.

Like that, we managed to catch our limit of twenty salmon. I remember how excited Danny was by the catch. We immediately took the fish back to his house and began filleting them. We selected a few fillets for our own dinner that night and wrapped the rest in a double layer of plastic wrap and waxed freezer paper. Danny then packed them into his freezer, equating their preciousness to the bars of gold stacked in the vault at Fort Knox. That night, we sat around a plug-in deep fryer on his picnic table and gorged on cubed fish.

I thought about that meal constantly as I drove back home from the UP. I was supposed to be readying myself for the upcoming trapping season, but over the last year I'd found myself getting depressed and disillusioned every time I was forced to think about trapping. For the past decade, I had devoted myself to studying the animals I trapped. I knew their habits the way that most people know their pets. That form of intimacy inevitably breeds love and respect, in the same way that the Native American tribes that most revered buffalo were those that spent the most time hunting them. But the thing I kept returning to in my mind was the notion of value. What, exactly, is an animal's life worth, and who is responsible for setting the price?

Consider a skunk. The market value of a skunk's pelt depends on a cryptic collection of economic factors and fashion trends as well as the color, size, density, and luster of the animal's fur. After the fur boom, this value was established at two or three dollars, absolute tops. But you couldn't just stop catching skunks, because they were a common by-catch species that inevitably turned up in traps set for fox and coyote. Complicating this was the fact that it was basically impossible to remove a live skunk from a trap without getting yourself sprayed. To avoid their wrath, you had to shoot them. The best way to do this was to hit the skunk in the heart with a .22 bullet, because then there was only about a 50 percent chance that the skunk would spray when it died. But a skunk's heart is not big, and you can't get too close when making the shot because you don't want to get sprayed while you aim. So hitting the heart was maybe a 50/50 proposition, which meant that there was a 75 percent chance that the skunk would spray on itself.

Since the animal ended up being dead anyway, I always figured that I had an obligation to skin it and sell it. To do this, I had to wash the hide in a bucket of gasoline in order to neutralize the odor. I remember a day when I was washing a skunk hide and realized that I was actually losing money on the animal due to the cost of the gasoline. Looking back, it's disturbing to imagine that an animal's life could achieve negative value.

What Matt and Danny had begun to achieve through hunting was something far more primal and self-contained. What they were doing transcended the notion of commerce. While I was heading into the woods in order to put fur coats into stores, they were heading into the woods to put food on their plates. It was an utterly simple equation. For them, the value of an animal was fixed. It did not change according to markets and trends. A 110-pound deer provided about thirty thousand calories of energy and five thousand grams of protein. Of course, that deer has a potent spiritual significance as well, but that potency was supported by the universal usefulness of its flesh. We need to eat to survive. We need to kill to eat.

After that trip, I began focusing my energies on a move to the Upper Peninsula. For that I needed cash, so I took a full-time job doing construction work. In the evenings and on the weekends I cut and split firewood and heaped it into a garage-sized mound across the street from my parents' house. By late summer I'd paid off the debts that I'd accrued while trapping and I'd put eighteen hundred dollars in the bank. I figured this amount could get me through until Christmas break, when I could come home and sell my mountain of firewood at high-dollar wintertime prices. When I shared this budget with my dad, he had just one question.

"What are you going to eat? You didn't really account for that."

"That's the point," I explained. "I'm gonna live off wild game."

He was incredulous. "You're going to attend classes *and* hunt and fish enough to feed yourself?" he asked.

"Well, not just me," I said. "There's Danny, too. And Matt Drost."

The three of us, along with another guy, secured a dilapidated four-bedroom house in Sault Sainte Marie that cost only $110 apiece in monthly rent. The paint on the place was so old that it hung to the structure in brittle flakes that reminded me of what it might look like if you glued potato chips to a vertical surface. The yard came furnished with a squatter who lived in a trailer on the alley side of the house. This guy poached our electricity from an outlet that you could access from the outside by reaching in through a fissure in the wall that was created when a third of the house slumped away from the main part.

The inside of the house was worse than the outside. The upstairs shower leaked through the living room ceiling in small rivulets that we captured in five-gallon buckets. We asked the landlord to fix this, and he eventually came over to apply an ineffectual thread of caulk no thicker than a strip of toothpaste. Eventually I bought a gallon of roofing tar and used a paint stirrer to apply it in strips about as wide as an adult's hand. This stopped the leaks with much authority, though the tar was slow to dry. Soon the bottoms of shampoo bottles had tar on them, and then all of the surfaces that the shampoo bottles touched had circles of tar on them as well. Even our bar of soap got tar on it, introducing us to the idea of dirty soap.

Living there, I enjoyed some of the best days of my life. While I don't intend to disparage the level of academic rigor required of students at Lake Superior State University, I can say that about 90 percent of our waking hours outside of the actual classroom were devoted to the issue of food acquisition. Luckily for us, the pink salmon spawning run coincided almost perfectly with the beginning of school. We crossed International Bridge to fish the Canadian side of the Sault Rapids with such frequency that the border patrol agents started asking us how the fishing was instead of asking where we were coming from and where we were going. We were each allowed to bring home two pink salmon per visit to Canada. One of these fish would feed one guy for about a day, so we should have only needed to fish three times a week. But our household soon had a reputation for serving fresh, wild-caught salmon, and we were inundated with nightly dinner guests. The result was that we consumed fish as fast as we caught them, no matter how many we caught, and we never managed to freeze a single ounce of salmon.

The lack of salmon in our freezer was a problem, for sure, though it was a refreshing one to have. Growing up, we rarely killed something and then ate it on the same day—unless it was the symbolic meal of a deer heart cooked on the morning it was shot. Instead, game

and fish were usually tucked away in the freezer for some special occasion or another, when we'd thaw a bunch out and share it with family friends. We kept game meat in a separate freezer, down in the
basement. Next to that freezer were the canning shelves, where we
stored produce from the garden and fruit from the U-pick blueberry
and raspberry farms that abounded around our home. My family
lived a weird double life. We had a hidden pioneer existence, with
wild meat and canned produce in the basement, while store-bought
veggies and frozen chicken breasts lived upstairs.

Because our family didn't rely entirely on game, it was sometimes
possible for us to overharvest. I remember a stretch of years when the
bullhead* population in our lake exploded. The water was really high
then, and in the early summer the fish were spawning inside every
submerged crack and crevice they could find near the shore: cracks in
seawalls, in the mouths of abandoned muskrat dens, inside the holes
of the cement blocks that neighbors used to support their fishing
docks. My brothers and I would go around with D-cell flashlights at
night in order to peer into these hiding places for fish; spawning bull-
heads are so aggressive that they'll hit a lure even if you're standing
within arm's reach of them. I remember one night when we caught
nine of them in a couple of hours. They all weighed around two to
three pounds. In the morning, we went through all the hassle of nail-
ing their heads to boards and stripping their skin off with end-cutting
pliers and then filleting them with Rapala knives. Then all the fillets
went into the freezer, which served as something akin to a fish and
game purgatory.

When something ended up in the freezer, it was up to our parents
to pull it out and cook it up. Whether or not that happened in a
prompt fashion depended on many variables, including how we la-

---

*Bullhead are very similar in appearance to catfish, and closely related taxonomically.

beled them, where in the freezer we put them, what else was in the freezer, and whether we had any big fish fries planned. I hate admitting it, but a lot of that stuff inevitably went to waste. Every year or so, we'd clean out the freezer and get rid of the freezer-burned stuff that was never used.

I now see this sort of behavior as an atrocity, the kind of offense that should be punished by having your hand nailed to a board, skinned with end-cutting pliers, and filleted. I refuse to hunt and fish with guys who routinely lose frozen game because "the freezer got unplugged" or because it wasn't wrapped properly and got freezer burn; that is, I refuse to hunt with guys who practice the freeze-it-and-forget-it wild game management strategy. There is no excuse for it. And while I hardly think that being poor is the only way to break such wasteful habits, I can say that my initial economically impoverished experiment with living off the land was like a form of shock therapy. Drost and Danny and I had inadvertently become a three-man tribe of hunter-gatherers. For us, the wild fish from the freezer had gone from being a treat to a daily necessity. As a result, the act of fishing took on a vital sense of immediacy. And our appreciation for the species that sustained us blossomed into something that resembled religion.

With all that said, we were still faced with two significant problems. One, we had an empty freezer; and two, we knew we couldn't live much longer on a diet of wild salmon. Besides the fact that we were getting awfully tired of it, there was also the issue of a deteriorating source. Salmon die after spawning, as everyone knows, and as the run progressed through September, the fish got continually nastier and nastier as they began to approach their inevitable demise. They were as silver as aluminum foil when they first showed up in the river, with

Danny and me with a catch of fish from Lake Superior,
laid out on our kitchen table in Sault Sainte Marie, Michigan.

pinkish, translucent flesh. But now their skin was getting as dark as a cigarette smudge and their flesh was the color of white bread that's been floating in the sink. Soon the only fish left were in such bad shape that you could catch them by hand—not that you'd want to.

What these problems meant for us was that our experiment in wild game living was threatened within just a couple of weeks of starting. And our blossoming tribe of hunter-gatherers was faced with hard times. When small-game season opened we tried to round out our diets with a miscellaneous assortment of ruffed grouse, snowshoe hares, woodcocks, and even beaver meat, but the difficulty of hunting them only stressed the importance of the one thing that was on all of our minds: whitetail deer.

The opening day of the archery season was about a week away, on October 1, and that date began to hang over our heads in the same all-important way that exam week hangs over the heads of normal students. The opener happened to fall on a Saturday that year, which meant we had a two-day weekend when we could hunt deer without having to tap into the tightly limited number of absences we were allowed before the school would start coming after us with disciplinary action.

Obviously, you don't just walk into the woods one day and kill a deer with an arrow. It takes massive amounts of preparation: locating hunting areas, scouting for sign, selecting places for tree stands, hours and hours of archery practice, tweaking and re-tweaking equipment. The first of these issues, a hunting area, had been addressed a year earlier when Danny and Drost secured hunting permission from a plaque-toothed, jovial farmer south of town whose property looked more like an untamed wetland than an area of agricultural production. He had a fallow field that stretched back a half mile from a county road and abutted a tract of state forest that was dominated by cedar swamp, beaver ponds, and dense stands of poplar. It was deep woods back there; at night, deer would pour into the field like sparrows coming into a spilled bag of popcorn in a shopping mall parking lot. At least they would do that up until a day or two after opening day. Then, having sensed trouble, they would mysteriously vanish back into the bush, where it was next to impossible to find them. Danny and Drost had watched it happen the year before, without managing to kill one first. They then went meatless until rifle season, a full six weeks later. Those were some lean times they weren't eager to repeat.

We set up three tree stands, one for each of us. Danny and Drost set theirs on the edges of the field, which weren't really edges at all because of the way that the forest was gradually reclaiming the land. Mine was way back behind the field, where a collection of deer trails emerged from some bedding areas and converged into a single super-trail that followed the edge of a marshy creek bed.

My father with a whitetail deer, late 1940s or early 1950s.
Southern Illinois.

My brothers fishing in front of our family home with
our maternal grandfather. Twin Lake, Michigan.

Cleaning bluegills at home with my brothers Danny (left) and Matt (center). My hands are on the right. Twin Lake, Michigan.

My father and me on Lake Michigan in the early 1980s. Matt is seated on the left.

A pair of red fox and some raccoons ready for market. Twin Lake, Michigan.

Danny (right) and me with a pair of whitetail deer killed in Newaygo County, Michigan.

A steelhead about to be released on Michigan's Muskegon River.

Carrying a young buck with my buddy Matt Drost (right). Tuskegee National Forest, Alabama.

My father and me with a
pair of Spanish mackerel.
Gulf Coast, Florida.

My father with a rare double
Robin Hood. He was no
bullshitter; this was legitimate.
Twin Lake, Michigan.

Ducks and geese. Clearwater
River, Montana.

My brother Matt butchering a bull elk in southwestern Montana.

My buddy Eric Kern and me with a pile of yellow perch. Canyon Ferry Reservoir, Montana.

An archery-killed cow elk. Madison Range, Montana.

My brothers and me, along with our friend Matt Moisan (far left), with a daily bag limit of Canada geese. Yellowstone River, Montana.

Danny with a bonefish. Yucatán Peninsula, Mexico.

My brothers and me with a freshly killed mule deer. Missouri Breaks, Montana.

The shack, with a bear ready to be butchered. Prince of Wales Island, Alaska. (Courtesy of Ron Boehme)

Butchering a caribou in the Alaska Range. Central Alaska. (Courtesy of Daniel J. Rinella)

Danny (left) and Matt (right) with a Dall ram.
Central Alaska.

Matt with his pack llamas, Timmy (left) and Haggy (right).
Southwestern Montana.

A ptarmigan that I
bagged with a .44
Magnum loaded
with birdshot.
Central Alaska.

Taking a rest after a turkey hunt. Southeastern Montana. (Courtesy of Randi Berez)

Packing out of turkey camp. Southeastern Montana. (Courtesy of Randi Berez)

Surfcasting. Fire Island, New York.

Butchering a moose with friends. Alaska Range, Alaska.

Floating out a load
of moose meat.
Alaska Range.
(Courtesy of Matt
Rafferty)

A pair of ptarmigan. Alaska's
North Slope.

A smallmouth bass.
Delaware River,
Pennsylvania.

Camp meat.
North Slope.

A late-season caribou
camp. Northern Alaska.

Wild boar meat.
Northern California.
(Courtesy of Dan
Doty)

Buffalo meat, sliced for
drying. Sonora, Mexico.
(Courtesy of Morgan
Fallon)

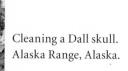

Cleaning a Dall skull.
Alaska Range, Alaska.

Danny's wife, Corrina, on her wedding day. (Courtesy of Daniel J. Rinella)

Katie's first halibut. Prince of Wales Island, Alaska.

Casting for salmon with my buddy Andrew Radzialowski (right). Southeastern Alaska. (Courtesy of Randi Berez)

Danny and me in Central Alaska. (Courtesy of Chris Flowers)

Bowfishing gar pike at the hot-water discharge on Muskegon Lake. Western Michigan. (Courtesy of Tracy Breen)

Remi Warren (left) and me with a Himalayan tahr from the glacial high country. South Island, New Zealand. (Courtesy of Dan Doty)

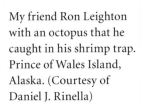

My friend Ron Leighton with an octopus that he caught in his shrimp trap. Prince of Wales Island, Alaska. (Courtesy of Daniel J. Rinella)

My family aboard a de Havilland Otter. Ketchikan, Alaska.

My son takes his first bite of wild game. Brooklyn, New York.

I spent the opening morning of archery season in that stand, shifting my weight from foot to foot and wishing that I'd rigged up some kind of seat. In the afternoon I found some distraction by marveling at a ruffed grouse that was working the area around my tree. It looked like a diminutive and cautious chicken as it scratched and pecked at the leaves on the ground and emitted a popping sort of cluck that wouldn't sound out of place if it were attributed to a piece of hardware in an outer-space movie. I'd be lying if I said that I didn't think about having this bird for dinner, but at the time I was worried about making noise that might scare away an unseen deer.

The grouse, a male, passed out of sight behind a cluster of trees and started to do something known as "drumming." They do this by beating their cupped wings against their bodies in order to emit a sound like that of an old lawn mower starting up. Presumably it's meant to announce their territory to other male grouse. It's their way of saying, "Back off, suckers!" Grouse are famously finicky about their drumming sites. They insist on logs or stumps that are about ten or twelve inches off the ground and centered in an area where there's about a sixty-foot radius of fairly open surveillance in any direction. It makes them easy to hear but extremely difficult to sneak up on, and it's possible to go your whole life without witnessing the scene. So I was obviously working my ass off in an effort to see it. I was leaning this way and that and getting down on my knees and climbing a little higher in my tree.

It's amazing that I didn't spook the buck that was headed my way. When I did register his presence, it wasn't so much that I saw him as felt him. Maybe it was a sound, maybe it was something in my peripheral vision, but suddenly I just knew he was somewhere off to my left. I froze in place and twisted my neck slowly around. The buck had a dark mane running down his back, an unusual though not unheard-of feature. His eight antler tines were like a tightly wrapped basket that would have been perfect for holding a cantaloupe. He was standing dead still about seventy yards away. Then his hoof came forward and he was moving again, heading toward me.

There were tremendous similarities between the way this buck was approaching and the way that the buck had approached all those years ago when I was hunting with my dad near Peacock, Michigan. He was going to pass by just about the same distance away from my tree. The animal was moving at the same speed. His body was about the same size. But there was a fundamental underlying difference now, because I was preparing to kill this animal for the specific purpose of feeding myself. This was not about pleasing my dad, or proving my mettle. This was not about fear. This was about food. I pulled back my bow and looked down the arrow. The specificity of my purpose made everything seem clear and straight. I could almost see that deer's heart—I could almost taste it, even—and my profound desire alone was enough to guide the arrow true. I saw a flicker as the fletch-

At our house in Sault Sainte Marie, 1994. Our motto was
"Burgers for lunch, steaks for dinner."

ing disappeared into the hide behind the deer's shoulder. The animal jumped almost straight up, then bounded forward and to the right and splashed through the creek. I heard the first couple of leaps but then the sound of the running stopped. Not faded away, but stopped dead. I then did as my dad always told me to do. I waited an hour before climbing down.

By then it was dark, so I had to use my flashlight. I walked until I hit water, and then continued on. The deer was lying just forty yards away, its hide looking black and slick with water. I approached its body quietly and I felt moved to do something that I'd never done before. I got down on my knees and buried my nose into the hair of its still warm neck and I breathed in its smell. I thanked it. I told it that it would be used well. And with respect. And soon.

|||||||||||||||||||||||||||||||||||||||||||||||||||||||||||||||||||||||||||||||||||||||||||||||||||||||||||||||

Tasting Notes: Black Bear

You eat one black bear and it tastes as bad as half-rotten fish, and then the next one tastes as good as blueberries. How this happens is hardly a mystery. The flavor of a particular bear has a lot to do with what the animal's been eating, and what the animal's been eating has a lot to do with opportunism and random chance. A friend of mine who lives near the hunting and fishing shack that my brothers and I own on Prince of Wales Island, in southeast Alaska, told me a story about a black bear that raided a workshop and consumed three gallons of bar-and-chain oil. Others have told me stories about black bears eating everything from Crayola crayons to rubber rafts to vinyl gas cans.* While I doubt that those substances improve the palatability of a bear's flesh, none of them is as deleterious to its taste as the more normal things that a hungry black bear is likely to come across in his wanderings. My brother Matt's buddy in Montana killed a black bear that was feeding on the bloated carcass of a cow. After skinning the bear, he found that he couldn't go near the meat without gagging. I've had similar though less dramatic experiences with coastal bears that have been feeding on spawned-out salmon. One time I prepared a coastal black bear's ham in a smoker that I'd borrowed from a buddy. The ham came out tasting just like fish, so I went over and accused my buddy of not properly cleaning his smoker after using it to make his last batch of smoked salmon. He informed me that he'd never put a fish in that smoker. I then looked at the forty pounds of meat that I'd pulled from that bear and knew I was in for a long haul of bad meals.

---

*At which point these substances kill the bear, I have no idea. A few bites of a rubber raft surely doesn't faze it. Gallons of gear oil might be a different story. But, for whatever reason, I picture that bear surviving, albeit with a horrible case of the shits.

While I do wish that all bears tasted great, the variability of their flesh makes hunting them all the more enjoyable. It's kind of like gambling, but instead of either winning or losing you've got the dichotomy of enjoying your meals or just enduring them. My first taste of bear meat was the former variety. It came from a bear that Danny killed in Michigan's Upper Peninsula. He and I took a chunk of meat from the bear's back leg and sprinkled it with salt and pepper and cooked it with carrots and potatoes in the oven. We liked it a lot better than any chunk of meat that we'd ever pulled from a whitetail deer.

The second black bear I ever ate was the first one I ever killed. It was a three-hundred-plus-pound bruiser that I shot in mid-April in Montana's Bitterroot Mountains. Back then, the state offered a free service of testing hunter-killed bear meat for the cysts of the roundworm *Trichinella spiralis*, which can cause the parasitic disease trichinosis. So, before eating any of the bear, I mailed in a golf-ball-sized chunk of the animal's tongue for analysis at a laboratory at Montana State University. I then went ahead and processed the bear's meat while I waited for the results. I turned the loins and upper rear legs into roasts, and still had eighty-seven pounds of trim left over for hamburger. My roommate worked at the meat counter of a local grocer, and he was kind enough to offer his assistance in processing the meat after hours so long as we kept it secret. After double-grinding all the burger, we wrapped it in two-pound packages using Styrofoam trays and plastic wrap coverings. A few days later, after getting news that the bear meat was indeed infected with the cysts of *Trichinella spiralis*, we started to wish that we'd done a better job of sanitizing the store's equipment.

Trichinosis is the reason you're supposed to cook pork to well done. The cysts of the roundworm are passed from one creature to the next through the consumption of infected flesh. Carriers in North America include a wide array of omnivores and carnivores, such as pigs, rats, mountains lions, walruses, bears, and, on occasion, humans. Symptoms include muscle pain, fever, swelling around the eyes, hemorrhaging under the nails, and, in rare cases, encephalitis and a number of neurological complications. Nowadays the condition has been effectively eliminated in the United States, thanks to strict U.S. Department of Agriculture guidelines that prohibit feeding animal flesh to commercially raised hogs. (Especially effective was the ban on feeding restaurant table scraps to hogs. The waste itself wasn't contaminated, but the rats and mice that got into it often were.) There are only a few dozen cases or so of trichinosis reported every year; of those, the vast majority are linked to black bear meat. In some counties in Montana, including the one where I killed the bear, 100 percent of all bears over the age of six are infected. My bear, according to analysis of the cementum annuli in its teeth, was seventeen.*

Along with the test results, the Montana Fish, Wildlife & Parks Commission issued me a notice that I was excused from the wanton waste laws that prohibit the wastage of game meat. I was free to toss the meat out if I wanted to. However, the guilt of discarding the bear's meat would have been much less tolerable to me than the risk of consuming it. So I did some research on cooking temperatures and bought a meat thermometer. (While USDA guidelines once suggested that pork be cooked to an internal temperature of 165 degrees, the advised temperature has now been reduced to 145 degrees.) I spent the next six months thrusting the prong of that thermometer into everything from sloppy joe mix to grilled loins. Soon I could tell the temperature of meat just by poking it with my finger. Now I don't even bother getting my bears tested. I just assume that they're infected and then proceed with caution.

The best black bear meat I've eaten has come out of Southcentral Alaska, specifically from the interior mountains where the bears don't have ready access to salmon. There a bear might start eating an almost exclusive

---

*Black bears in captivity have lived into their thirties, but they have much shorter life spans in the wild. In fact, it's rare to find bears much older than ten. This seventeen-year-old bear was certainly pushing the limits of the species.

diet of berries in the month of June and then continue doing so until it goes down for hibernation in mid- to late October. Their meat is uncorrupted by weird stuff like rotten meat and spawned-out salmon. People I serve it to usually declare it to be one of their favorite wild meats. Comparisons to beef pot roast are common, both in terms of flavor and texture.

But the best thing about these bears is their fat. The blueberries give it a purplish tint, and I swear to God it tastes almost sweet. It's so good that you can melt it and spread it on toast like butter. Or, better yet, you can render the oil and fry cubes of bear meat in it. Another good thing is to use it for making french fries. Done properly, they come out as good as McDonald's fries used to taste before they stopped frying them in beef lard as a frying medium. The last time I killed a black bear, in Alaska's Chugach Range, I hauled off a few sacks of the fat and brought them home to New York. I cut the fat into one-inch cubes and placed a few handfuls of them into a large heavy pot. Set over low heat, the cubes started giving up a fine, clear oil. A couple of hours later, the cubes had turned into little wafers that resembled pork rinds floating in a bath of oil. By the time I was done adding the cubes, there were three gallons of rendered oil in the pot. I strained out the rinds and then poured the vat of oil through a filter of cheesecloth and into glass Mason jars. It was as clear as olive oil while warm, though it turned white like packed snow once it had cooled. I labeled each jar with a strip of masking tape that said BEAR OIL. I burned through the oil quickly at first, both by giving it away and using it myself, but then my usage slowed to nothing once I was down to a single jar. The jar lives in the front of my fridge, waiting for a special occasion. In the meantime, it serves as a reminder to kill another fat bear as soon as possible. It's like a shopping list, except it tastes better.

CHAPTER SEVEN

Playing with Food

★

WHEN YOU'RE FIELD dressing an animal, a practice known less delicately as gutting, you have to split open the rib cage and reach inside and grab the heart and sever its moorings. For anyone who's prone to pondering the meaning of things, it's hard to do this without coming to the realization that you're engaged in very serious business. At a time, it was impossible for humans to live without coming face-to-face with this kind of nastiness. Back then, there was no hiding from the fact that we have to kill to eat. Nowadays, however, we've devised all sorts of clever mechanisms that enable us to avoid this reality. I'm thinking of grocery stores, restaurants, that sort of thing. But perhaps the strangest manifestation of our increasing lack of stomach has to be catch-and-release fishing.

Just to be clear, catch-and-release fishing amounts to poking a hole into a fish's face and exhausting it, then letting it go because you don't want to hurt it. When I say the practice is strange, I'm saying that its initial invention must have been the result of some freakish anomaly. If you rolled back human history to the very beginning and let our species have another go at it, we'd definitely rediscover such things as dancing, hunting, the benefits of shelter, transoceanic shipping, drug abuse, restaurants, and maybe even online dating. But catch-and-release would almost certainly join the ranks of high-heeled shoes and wearing your pants down around your hips so that you've got to walk funny in order to keep them from falling down. The circumstances that delivered these ideas just wouldn't be replicated.

Thanks to its strangeness, I often find myself explaining, both to myself and others, how I got into catch-and-release fishing and then how I got away from it. The answer to the first part of that question has to do with steelhead, a large and anadromous strain of rainbow trout.* Big ones can weigh over twenty pounds, sometimes way over. They are fast—"like an F-16," says one fishing writer,† "whereas a salmon is like a B-52"—and beautiful. They have a dark upper half with black spots, a blush-colored lateral line, and a chrome belly. While steelhead are native to the Pacific Rim, from California to Alaska's Aleutian Islands to Siberia's Kamchatka Peninsula, they are so admired that they've been introduced to waterways well outside their native range. They were first introduced into the Great Lakes region back in 1876, the same year that General George Armstrong Custer was killed and mutilated at the Battle of the Little Bighorn.

Growing up, I didn't hear too much about steelhead unless it was April or May. Those were the primary months when breeding-age fish would leave the vast sanctuary of Lake Michigan and head inland along the rivers and streams that coursed through the interior of the state. They'd pop up here and there. Maybe a friend would find a half-dead steelhead that had taken a few wrong turns and ended up in a drainage ditch along the side of the road, or maybe his older

---

*An anadromous fish lives its life in salt water and then returns to its freshwater natal stream in order to spawn. Salmon are the most commonly known species that employs this life history. People often use the word *anadromous* when describing salmon (and steelhead) in freshwater ecosystems such as the Great Lakes, though the proper term for that is *adfluvial*—which describes fish that live in lakes and migrate into rivers and streams to spawn. Some anadromous fish, such as many species of salmon, spawn only once and then die. That's called *semelparity*. Steelhead, on the other hand, can spawn multiple times throughout their life span. That's called *iteroparity*.
†The writer is Pete Thomas, though he was quoting fishing guide Jeff Zennie.

brother would get busted by a warden for spearing a steelhead where the beavers always dammed up a culvert under the railroad tracks along Cedar Creek. But mostly the fish maintained a high level of secrecy and discretion.

In fact, I never even touched a live steelhead until I was fourteen years old. It happened on the last day of May, while Danny and I were camping on the White River. We were there because we'd gotten into trouble with our parents a week earlier for lying about something that we shouldn't have lied about. As punishment, we were forbidden from going anywhere besides work and school. But then Memorial Day weekend came around and our mom started to feel sorry for us and weighed in on our behalf. She convinced our dad that it should be permissible for us to take a three-day canoe trip down the White River since it would be nearly impossible for us to get into a similar kind of trouble there. We launched our yellow fiberglass canoe below the dam in Hesperia and started floating downstream.

Along the way we fished for the small resident strains of rainbow trout that tended to hang out in the seams where deep holes met faster-moving currents. For us, in that area, a good-sized one of these trout was ten inches long and weighed about a third of a pound. So imagine how excited we were when we glanced over the gunwale to see a large spawning bed beneath thigh-deep fast-moving water. The bed was four or five feet in diameter. All the algae and sediment had been scrubbed away from its gravel so that it looked as bright as the lighted window of a house at night. Four or five steelhead, each of them big like the blades of our canoe paddles, stood out against the gravel as clearly as people standing in those windows.

The fish bolted as we passed overhead, but that hardly stopped us from yelling and whooping and saying "holy shit" as we paddled our canoe to the river's left bank. We dragged the canoe onto a muddy beach and then walked back upstream and climbed a high riverbank where we could sit and watch the bed. At dark, the fish still hadn't returned. We went back to our canoe, unloaded it, and then laid out our sleeping bags not far from a No Trespassing sign.

In the morning the fish were back. Danny had swapped out his light trout line with heavier monofilament, and he tied on a fly of brightly colored yarn that was meant to resemble a cluster of fish eggs. He cast upstream and beyond the bed, gave a couple of cranks on his reel, and then—boom!—he lifted his rod tip and was tight onto a fish. The fish booked downriver and we chased it. A few bends later and we hauled a large male steelhead up onto a gravel bar.

Even though we killed and gutted that fish, and then tied it to a cord and dragged it behind our canoe for about twenty miles, and then had our dad weigh it (sixteen pounds, even though it was gutted and a little dried out!), and then brined it and smoked it and ate it, I still like to blame that fish for my eventual and temporary conversion to a catch-and-release angler. The attention that Danny and I got for catching it was far greater than anything we'd ever gotten for catching a muskrat or a snapping turtle or even for shooting a deer. Our old man was so proud of us for catching a big steelhead that he actually put our grounding on probationary status. He told his buddies about our fish. Then his buddies came around and asked for more details. In fact, we talked and bragged about that fish to various friends and neighbors and relatives for the next week. We were heroes of the angling sort, which is a good sort of hero to be.

From that day on, I considered steelhead to be worth going after. First I chased them intermittently for a period of about five years. I might catch and kill one or two every spring and get pretty excited about it. Later, around the mid-nineties, there was a sort of perfect storm of developments in my life that began to change my perspective on the fish. Those developments were spurred primarily by the low fur prices of the mid-nineties, which caused me to shut down my trapping enterprise and move to the Upper Peninsula to hunt for food with my brother Danny while we took classes at LSSU. During that semester I'd come to the decision that if I couldn't be a professional trapper then I'd at least become a professional outdoor writer. This conviction resulted in some irony, as it caused me to leave the UP's great hunting and fishing behind in order to transfer to a college that offered an English degree with a writing emphasis but little in the way of outdoor opportunities.*†

I begrudgingly packed up my bags and moved downstate in January 1995, thinking that I'd finish college and then move right back to the UP. Regardless of my future plans, leaving made me feel like the worst kind of traitor. I felt as though I was abandoning my newfound tribe of hunter-gatherers and pissing on everything that we had stood for during that wonderful four months.

I moved in with a bunch of guys in Grand Rapids and signed up for classes at my third small college, this time Grand Valley State University. Soon after I settled in, I was contacted by a journalist with the *Detroit News* who was writing a story about the hard times that had befallen the state's fur trappers. We spent a day hanging out together and doing an interview. Then a photographer took me for a drive and had me pretend to set a beaver trap in a marsh that probably hadn't seen a beaver in two hundred years. The story was titled "Trapping Has Become a Lost Art, but Many Aren't Sad." It only reconfirmed what I already knew to be true, that trappers like myself were a dying breed and civilized Americans are hardly crying about it. But some-

---

*Full disclosure: There was a girl involved in my decision as well. Let's just say that it was an additional deciding factor, or at least a deal sweetener. We eventually broke up, and she now has two beautiful children and a husband who seems like a solid guy.
†LSSU did offer a BA in English, but at the time it was a program that focused way too heavily on old books. Or at least that was my opinion back then. Particularly irksome was the Shakespeare class I took there. That writer's reliance on double entendres and mistaken identities reminded me too much of the sitcom *Three's Company*.

how knowing this still heightened my sense that there was a massive hole in my life that I'd spent an entire decade digging. I sat around wondering to myself, what the hell does an ex-trapper do all winter in Grand Rapids?

The answer, I soon found out, was steelhead. As it happened, I suddenly found myself living amid some of the primest steelhead habitat in the Great Lakes. And this area didn't just get the spring runs of steelhead that I mentioned earlier. Here, in the Lower Peninsula, where the winters were much milder and less icy, the rivers also got runs of a rogue element of the steelhead population known as winter-run steelhead. These fish come upstream from Lake Michigan as early as October, November, or December. Everything about them is a little mysterious. It's not clear what prompts them to leave the protection of the Great Lakes for the relative vulnerability of the rivers in the first place. And once they get there, it's not entirely clear what they do. They mill around, and come and go, and appear and disappear and reappear. Think of them as the fish equivalent of a guy who begins making sporadic visits to the location of an out-of-town wedding a couple of months in advance of the other guests.

While I don't want to say that catching steelhead in the spring is easy, it's definitely not as hard as catching them in the winter. Either case can be likened to hitting a bull's-eye, though the wintertime bull's-eye is only about a fifth as big and a lot farther away. Guys who excelled at catching them were often referred to as "steelheaders," a term meant to convey respect and admiration. You might be at a birthday party or some such affair and overhear two guys conversing quietly about a third guy across the room. Pointing toward him discreetly, one might say to the other, "Now *that* guy's a steelheader."

Nowhere was the admiration for steelheaders more pronounced

than it was among my circle of friends at LSSU. It was the kind of school where students had a lot of pride. Not that raucous strain of sports pride, like at the big football schools in the South (though LSSU does have a popular hockey team); and not academic pride, like at places like Princeton or Yale. It was more of a geographical pride. Kids were proud to live in that tough wilderness setting, and the best way to prove your mettle was through achievements in the wild. One of the top achievements was to catch a lot of steelhead at times when other guys couldn't find them. Outsmarting these elusive fish in the big and cold rivers required toughness, cunning, intelligence, and the good kind of craziness. Danny even went so far as to have a steelhead tattooed on his upper arm. And while I know this will make me sound ridiculous, I was in large part motivated to catch steelhead because I knew I would be respected by the people whom I respected. Suddenly I could one-up my buddies in the Far North by catching piles of winter-run steelhead while they got drunk on half-frozen Boone's Farm while fishing five-inch perch through the ice.

One of the best-known steelhead rivers in my area happened to be the eponymous river that flowed through downtown Grand Rapids. However, the grandness of the Grand River's rapids had long ago been subdued by a number of dams. The most prominent of these was the Sixth Street Dam, which served as one of the focal points for urban waterfront traffic. Here passersby could watch the river actually do something—fall over a head-high ledge—rather than simply flow by. Adding to the draw was a public parking lot on the west side of the dam where the state had installed an artfully designed fish ladder to help migratory species bypass the structure. The lot saw traffic from guys coming and going from the nearby rehab clinic as well as guys coming and going from selling their blood plasma at a biological services facility. You also had more standard traffic, such as people walking their dogs and people on lunch break who parked in the lot and ate their sandwiches.

I joined the fray at Sixth Street Dam, though with a different set of motivations. The same structure that provided visual entertainment for passersby presented an annoyance to migratory fish. A steelhead that was headed upriver might only spend a moment or two at any specific point along the forty miles of river between the rapids and Lake Michigan, but it was sure to stop at the dam and linger around for hours or days as it tried to figure out how to get past it.

Because the Grand River is deep and dark, especially in the winter, you couldn't just look into the water to see if the fish had shown up. Instead you had to put on a pair of waders and climb in and make a few casts. The only problem with this strategy was that it was incapable of yielding negative results. If you cast into the river and hooked a fish, you had a positive—you knew that at least one fish was there. But if you cast into the river and didn't hook a fish, all you really knew was that you didn't hook a fish. This left you wanting to go back the next day and try again to make sure.

I did quite a bit of this during the months of January and February, always hopeful that a bunch of steelhead would suddenly materialize in the river and fulfill my dreams of being a steelhead hero. While my initial explorations didn't turn up many fish, they did reveal a mysterious and dangerous world that existed beneath the water. The danger came from the dam, which is known as a low-head, or overflow dam. It looks like a long waterfall with the water spilling over with such velocity that you could ride over it on a boogie board. Where the falling water hit was a roiling and boiling pit of froth about as wide as a backyard swimming pool. Just downstream from the pit was a narrow reeflike jumble of mostly submerged concrete slabs that had all kinds of bent reinforcement rods sticking out of them. The reef ran more or less the entire length of the dam except for a large gap in the middle known as the center run. Through this run, the roiling wash flowed out unimpeded as a fast and deep river. Rumor had it that this was the best place to fish.

Getting to the center run wasn't too tricky when the water was low—say below five thousand cubic feet per second, as reported by the U.S. Geological Survey—but it was a real challenge when the water levels came up after it rained or after a lot of snow melted off. Then you had to navigate the completely submerged reef of concrete slabs while trying to avoid getting tangled on the rebar or slipping into the cracks between the slabs. With the fast current, it made me think of trying to walk a strand of barbed wire in high winds. After a cold snap, you had to add to this the threat of the ice sheets that came spilling over the dam.

Keep all that in mind for a moment as I explain another aspect of Sixth Street Dam. Because of the high volume of passersby, it was impossible for there to be any secrets about what was happening at the dam. If someone hauled a fish out of the river, word spread. The next day, that fish would be replaced by ten additional anglers who were all intent on catching one just like it. This problem wouldn't have been so bad if it weren't for the fact that high water levels tended to attract more steelhead at the same time that they limited the number of places in the river where fishermen could stand while trying to catch them. Suddenly the few good places near the safety of the river's banks were so full of fishermen that the guys actually had to synchronize their casts in order to avoid banging their rod tips together and crossing their lines. It was mayhem, pure and simple.

Such was the case in late January when I came down to the river one morning when the flows were over six thousand. There I was reminded of the fishing writer John Gierach's observation that there are only two kinds of anglers: those in your party and the assholes. Here the assholes had the place completely plugged up. There wasn't a single worthwhile place to stand along the entire bank of the river. Meanwhile, thanks to the raging level of water, the reef of slabs running out toward the center run was conspicuously absent of fishermen.

As I stood on the bank I pondered the idea of just going back home rather than fighting with the crowds. Screw it, I thought. But then I thought, screw *that*. I'm a steelheader. So I walked down to the river's edge, pardoned my way through the line of fishermen, and began making my way out along the reef as if I'd done it a thousand times in similar conditions. A few of the guys were clearly pissed that they had to hold their casts while I worked my way out in front of them. But still I pushed on.

By the time I was clear of the fishermen along the bank it was obvious that I couldn't go any farther. The water was over my waist and lapping at the top of my waders. It was flowing so fast that I had to lean into it at a pronounced angle. But all I could think about was what a jackass I'd look like if I turned around and made them stop casting while I retreated. The one thing that was clear was that I couldn't stay put. The current was pushing my boot and causing it to slide. To keep my footing, I had to move one way or another. I inched my boot forward into the river and felt around for the next stable place to set it.

There are rumors around Sixth Street Dam of guys falling into the overflow wash and getting Maytagged to death, or falling the other way and being sucked under by the fast current. I thought of this over the next few minutes as I forged ahead. By then I figured that I had to make it all the way to the center run, where I could stand on a familiar slab of concrete that was pitched against the current and offered a good place to wedge my boot for stability.

I was shaking from exertion when I finally hit that slab. Once I got my balance I managed to glance behind me to see that everyone was following my predicament with some level of amusement. They were fishing and milling about, as usual, but they were definitely tuned into what I was doing. I decided that the only way to save face was to make a couple of casts and continue the charade as if this were all part of the plan. My shenanigans had devolved into performance, pure and simple.

In that river, the rig to use was a fly rod and reel loaded with thirty-pound-test shooting line. You would use a nail knot to join about eight feet of twelve-pound-test monofilament to that, and then a surgeon's knot to join an eight-pound test tippet. Before stepping into the water I'd tied on an egg-pattern fly made from chartreuse yarn. Now all I had to do was pinch on enough lead split shot to get my fly down toward the bottom in the fast water. I hucked the fly up into the wash of the falls and gave it plenty of slack so the fly could sink. As the current pushed the fly down I tightened the line and followed it with my rod tip so that I could feel the split shot bouncing along the river's bed. Once it passed me up, the current lifted the fly to the surface. All in all the cast resembled the swing of a pendulum.

My first few shots explored the distant edge of the gap, and from there I moved my casts closer and closer until I was fishing almost directly beneath my own toes. When the line stopped mid-swing through a cast, my initial thought was that I'd snagged on a piece of rebar. But no sooner did I tighten my line against the snag than an outraged slab of chrome rose out of the swirling froth. The steelhead executed a few lateral twists in the air before the belly of the line was able to exit the water. Then he shot down through the gap, yanked off a bunch of line, jumped a few more times, and booked thirty yards downriver.

At that point the fish was as good as gone. To chase him downriver was impossible, as pulling my foot away from its position in the rock would be akin to sticking my head underwater and inhaling a lungful. If the fish had been thinking, he would have kept going downriver until he stripped off all the line and I had to snap him off. But fish don't think, or at least they don't think like that. Suddenly he turned and ran right back upstream. He passed through the gap again and up into the froth. The swirling currents must have tired him quickly, because soon his head was shaking doggedly and I gained a bit of line. Lifting my rod, I was able to pull him close to me so that he was lolling at the water's surface with his face tilted up into dry air. It was a good-sized male, at least twelve pounds.

I glanced behind me. Just about everybody there, the pedestrians and the fishermen, were staring at me. I felt a childish sense of pride, not much different from the pride you feel when you walk into a bar with some good-looking girls. It was the pride of having something that other people wanted. Even though I knew it was a stupid way to feel, I felt it anyway and I luxuriated in the feeling.

My instinct was to hook an index finger through the fish's gill plate so that I had a death grip on it. But I knew there was no way I was going to make it back to the bank with the added burden of a fish. So instead I reached over and popped the hook free from its mouth. The steelhead vanished with a flap of its tail and a splash. If this escapade of mine had devolved into a performance, the movements of the liberated fish had elevated it to the level of performance art, or at least it had vindicated my stupidity. I was smiling wildly, which camouflaged my primary concern with getting some dry land under my boots. I carefully turned toward the shore and took a step in the direction of the bank. I was now a catch-and-release angler.

Not that I altogether stopped killing steelhead right then and there. Instead I began to do something like a light-beer version of catch-and-release. I'd go out and catch a steelhead and run a piece of parachute cord through its gill plate and tie it to a rock. Then I'd wade back into the river and catch a few more and let them go just for the heck of it. Soon I found myself reversing this process. I'd catch a couple and let them go, then maybe keep one for meat. By and by, I would let a couple of fish go and then never get around to keeping one at all.

Releasing fish, I found, offered me a new way of interacting with nature. Until then, I had been an exclusively extraction-based guy. I went into the woods or water with the intention of getting something useful—usually something that could be sold or eaten. To me, the kill was as essential to the acts of hunting and fishing as purchasing was to the act of shopping. But by releasing that fish instead of killing it, I found that it was possible to be thrilled by a different part of the process.

Of course, no serious catch-and-release fisherman would ever say that he releases fish as a way getting a fresh perspective on the process

Me releasing a female steelhead at the Sixth Street Dam in Grand Rapids, Michigan.

of fishing. Instead he'd probably explain it in terms of preserving the resource. He'd say that he gets more pleasure from catching a fish than eating it, and once you eat it you can't catch it again. That's true enough, but I've always been suspicious of anyone who claims that as their singular reason for releasing fish. I think of it as a form of shorthand for things that are more complicated, or even less flattering. I know a guy who cites preservation as his reason, though one day he confided to me that he actually just doesn't like to eat fish. Another acquaintance of mine cites preservation when I know for a fact that he's too squeamish to handle and clean a dead fish.

My own reasoning was certainly complicated, so much so that I can't fully explain it. At some level, I'm sure I viewed the act of releasing fish as a form of contrition. There was definitely a connection in my mind—or reverse connection, as it were—between killing upward of a thousand furbearing mammals for money and then spending money in order to let other creatures live. And while one might argue that you can do a better job of letting things live by not catching them in the first place, you can't *actively* let them live until you've had a chance to kill them.

During my catch-and-release phase, I filled a photo album with snapshots of me posing with steelhead, the fish usually held at the water's surface in order to give a visual display of my intent. I also maintained a redundant system of chronicling every fish I let go with crosshatched tallies scratched into the dash of my van and marked on a card in my wallet. I detailed the particulars of these fish in a dedicated notebook and I scrapbooked the photos. The system was remarkably similar to the way I recorded the activities of my trapping business, except there was no business here. Rather, I was intent on owning the survival of the fish in the same way that I'd once owned the fur of muskrats. I learned how to take possession of a fish through its release. Two winters after letting my first steelhead go, I was proud to say that I scored forty-three hatch marks in a four-month period. I bragged about it the way some guys will brag about money.

Killers of fish select their favorite species according to edibility; they generally like the same fish that you might see on a restaurant menu, such as salmon, halibut, and walleye. Releasers of fish, however, don't give a damn about edibility. More interested in rarity and sporting qualities, they often admire fish that are too muddy or too boney or too mushy to be of much value at suppertime. I'm talking about brown trout, largemouth bass, tarpon, those sorts of fish. In fact, one of the greatest darlings of the catch-and-release fisherman is the bonefish, a species that many American anglers consider to be practically inedible.*

They aren't very attractive, either. An ichthyologist might describe bonefish as elongate, fusiform, and slightly compressed; your average Joe might say they are hoglike and inelegant, with a mouth shaped like a rechargeable handheld vacuum cleaner. But they've got a lot going for them outside of taste and looks, at least in an angling sense. For one thing they live in fun places; a guy fishing for bonefish can usually look up from the task at hand to see a palm tree and a white sand beach and possibly a woman in a bikini. Think the Bahamas, the Seychelles, Christmas Island, the Florida Keys, places like that.

They are also exceedingly fun and difficult to catch. Pound for pound, bonefish are considered by many to be the fastest and strongest fish on the planet. The bonefish's scientific name is *Albula vulpes,* or "white ghost," and many related and flowery nicknames have been

---

*A major exception to this rule is the indigenous fishermen of Hawaii. They call the fish *o'io* and frequently use them in traditional preparations such as fish cakes.

bestowed upon them: "phantoms of the flats," "ghosts of the flats," "silver ghosts," "silver phantoms," "silver shadows." These apparition-like names come from the fact that a bonefish's coloration—they resemble the brushed aluminum on the bottom of a beer can—makes them extremely challenging to see in their preferred environs of intertidal flats, where clear, sunlit water lies in a shallow layer over a dappled white seafloor.

Rather than being a detriment, the difficulty of spotting a bonefish is celebrated by anglers. You have to locate the fish visually in order to best catch them, and that requires concentration and acute attention to detail. Once located, a bonefish needs to be stalked like game. You need to get within casting distance, then land a fly close enough that the fish can see it but not so close that the disturbance of the line hitting the water scares the fish away. Once the bonefish is hooked, it'll take off so fast that the line will rip through the water with an electric zip. The whole package of this experience is so great that the fish deserves a pardon once it is captured.

Or so goes the theory, which Danny and I accepted without reluctance when we decided to head for Mexico's Yucatán Peninsula in order to catch one. Neither of us had ever been to Mexico, nor had we ever laid eyes on a bonefish, but we'd been inspired again and again by a Page-a-Day fly-fishing calendar with a strong tropical emphasis. Every week or so offered some badass photo of a guy standing in warm-looking water while gripping a rocket-shaped bonefish. We bought a couple of books about bonefish, including Randall Kaufmann's *Bone-fishing with a Fly*, and read plenty of sentences such as this one: "A bonefish mirage can suddenly transform into reality and just as quickly dissolve into illusion. Bonefish are indeed the phantoms of the flats." Soon we'd convinced ourselves that a fisherman wasn't worth a damn unless he'd tangled with and released this particular quarry.

When we conceived of the idea, Danny had been living with me for a month in order to save on rent while he fished and worked on applications for graduate programs in freshwater ecology. In our spare moments, we began supplementing the knowledge we'd gleaned from our calendar and books by making calls to fly-fishing shops that sold saltwater gear. Such calls were hardly helpful. I usually just got some naysayer or another who would speculate that our plan to backpack and hitchhike up and down the Yucatán would yield zero bonefish and would probably end with us dead in the jungle.

We bought our tickets and began tying flies. A few days before we left, we assembled a hodgepodge of gear on the floor and began filling two backpacks. We had flannel bedsheets, a stainless steel cooking pot, a tent, two plates and two cups, a change of clothes each, rain jackets, toiletries, basic fishing tools and tackle, two fly rods apiece, and a camp stove that could burn just about any petroleum-based fuel you threw at it. We pooled our funds into a four-hundred-dollar kitty that might, just maybe, get us through the month.

We landed in Cancún, took a cab to the bus station, and slept on benches outside while we waited for a southbound bus. We boarded early in the morning and rode to the town of Tulum. The streets near the bus station were lined with corrugated shacks where they sold chickens that were split down the spine, grilled, and then chopped into pieces between the blade of a machete and a tree stump. European backpackers with dark tans and tribal tattoos tried to sell handmade jewelry and joints to European backpackers who were less tanned and less tattooed.

We paid a nightly rate for a thatched hut on the south edge of town so we had somewhere to stash our stuff, then we wandered around drinking beer and eating chicken. In the morning we picked up our stuff and bought a stash of food and eight gallons of fresh water. We started walking south with our packs on our backs and eight pounds of water in each hand. We were headed down a dirt lane that followed a narrow peninsula separating the open Caribbean from a large saltwater lagoon. The road ran about forty miles and ended at a small lobster fishing village called Punta Allen. Our plan was to camp somewhere in the middle.

We were hoping to thumb a ride, but the few cars that happened along were already full of people or else the drivers ignored us. The trip took on a menacing quality, as it always strikes me as an act of hostility when you're hitchhiking and someone drives by at a slow speed and makes eye contact with you without picking you up. My mood was lifted significantly when I stumbled across the first bone-fish that either of us had ever seen. It was lying dead on the side of the road, about the size of a hoagie roll. It had been there long enough that the body inside the skin had begun to shrink away, leaving the skin dry and crinkly. We debated whether we should regard this as a good omen or a bad one, but we could only agree that it was a pretty damn weird one.

Eventually a guy hauling limes and bananas in the back of a Japanese-made pickup stopped long enough for us to jump in. We passed through a checkpoint and entered the Sian Ka'an, a United Nations–sponsored biosphere reserve that stretches almost all the way to Belize and encompasses about 1.3 million acres of Caribbean coastline. It is home to lagoons, monkeys, Mayan ruins, peccaries and jaguars, two kinds of crocodiles, and some 350 species of birds. We bumped along until we hit a narrow place in the peninsula a little more than half the way to the end. To the east, waves hit a long, fairly straight beach. To the west was the saltwater lagoon, barely visible through a fifty-yard-wide, seemingly impenetrable band of mangroves.

We banged on the window to let the driver know we wanted out. Then Danny and I ducked into the palms on the sea side of the road and looked for a good place to camp. Picking a campsite in unfamiliar territory is tricky. You want a site that is tucked away and hidden, but not so hidden that you look like you're running from the law. We eventually found a place with suitable anchoring points to string two hammocks that we'd bought in Tulum. Then we stashed our packs, strung our rods, and headed into the belt of mangroves.

Mangroves have thick, green, waxy leaves. The branches grow in a tightly interwoven way, and walking through them reminds me of trying to crawl through the wires on a window screen. We twisted and wrestled through the tangles, and our clothes became streaked with orange slashes from a staining liquid that rubs off when you touch the tree's limbs. About halfway through, I was stung on the arm by a worm about the size of a cigar butt with orange spikes coming out of its back. It hurt like hell.

"What the . . . Dammit!" I yelled.

"What happened?" said Danny.

"I just got nailed by a worm that's, like . . ." As I said it, the worm dropped from his mangrove perch and disappeared under the water.

We continued on. By the time we reached the edge of the mangroves the bite had swelled to the size of a 35-mm film canister. I thought about going back in and searching for the worm, so Danny would have something to show to the doctors if I died, but I didn't want to face those mangroves again.

The water in the lagoon looked white or gray or blue depending on the depth. On average it was about calf-deep, not counting the claylike muck that we sank into, which made it about knee-deep. Danny went north up the edge of the lagoon and I went south. I'd read how bonefish will spit streams of water from their mouths in order to flush shrimps and crabs from their hiding places in the mud, and how this action creates little golf-ball-sized divots in the bottom. I wondered if those were the golf-ball-sized divots that I was seeing just about everywhere I looked.

In hindsight I can't remember exactly if I saw it or heard it first. I feel as though I heard it, the sound of someone dipping their finger into a bathtub and wagging it back and forth. Or maybe I saw it first, the appearance of a tail fin sticking out of the water and wagging about. The tail fin was connected to a bonefish rooting about in water too shallow to contain its whole body. More fish were behind it. I fumbled with my rod and peeled off some line. Tied to the end was a type of fly known as a Crazy Charlie. It looked like a little brown shrimp made of yarn, with eyeballs made from the ball-chain that people associate with military dog tags. I landed the fly about five feet in front of the fish and he zipped forward to grab it. He then zipped off to my left so fast that the line made a sound like ripping newsprint and cast a rainbow-colored mist in the air. After two or three minutes I had the fish in my hand. A few seconds after that, it was free.

Days and days went by, and I began to understand that fly-fishing for bonefish while sleeping in a hammock strung between coconut palms leaves you with a lot of time on your hands. In order to see the fish you want a high and bright sun, which means that conditions are ideal only about four or five hours a day—say from 10 A.M. to 3 P.M., maximum. Of course, you can try your luck during the morning and evening, but then you risk stumbling upon fish and scaring them without ever realizing they were there. That wouldn't be so bad if you had endless water available to search in. But Danny and I were limited to those areas that we could reach on foot, so we had to be conservative with the available fish and pursue them only during optimal hours.

There were things we needed and wanted to do besides fishing, like swimming or napping or collecting firewood or climbing coconut palms to get food and drink. But we still had a lot of time to lie around and think about things. One of the things I thought about was whether Danny and I were completely nuts for spending a month camping in the sand while trying to catch a fish that we didn't want to eat. I tried to think of similar human behaviors, like the way people will travel halfway around the world just to look at a piece of art. They'll do it for the visual experience alone, without needing to take any part of the object with them. But then I thought that this wasn't a very good comparison, because we weren't just coming to look at bonefish. We were coming to catch them and touch them as well. It was more like traveling around the world in order to scratch a mark into a painting and then buff the mark away.

What added to this confusion was that we'd quickly gotten into the habit of supplementing our diet with fish. This was partly out of necessity: We had to conserve our rice and beans. And it was partly out of taste: We got sick of rice and beans. So whenever we were done chasing bonefish and letting them go, we'd head off in search of other fish to eat. We found a place where we could snag mullet by stringing a bunch of hooks together and dragging them through the schools. We found a few places where we could catch snapper by casting into pondlike openings that formed near the edges of the mangroves. We found deep channels in the lagoon where we could catch an array of small jacks and grunts. Sometimes I'd cut off a strip of tail flesh from a fish and put that on a hook and cast it out from our camp at night with the hopes of catching something bigger.

After dark we'd sit around, barefoot and bare-chested, frying fillets of fish in a pan over the stove. As we got grubbier and more weathered looking and more bitten up by flies, I began to think about how primal we were becoming: two filthy-haired guys by a fire with fish bones and coconut husks scattered about, one of the guys sporting a weird-looking welt from a worm bite. I liked the feeling of it, how we'd stripped our lives to primitive, bare essentials. The weirdest

Danny resting in his hammock at one of our many bonefish camps.
Yucatán Peninsula, Mexico.

thing was that we'd devolved into this primal state by trying to gather caloric fuel to enable our efforts at participating in an activity that was entirely abstract and modern, if not slightly sadistic: using a certain species of fish as a plaything, as though it were some type of living golf ball.

While I tried hard to put the irony and absurdity of our situation out of my head, I found it hard to do. My focus continually drifted away from our supposed task at hand—catch-and-release fishing for bonefish—and drifted toward the supplementary activity of food acquisition. I wondered if there was a way to cook the little crablike organisms that scurried nervously in and out of the thumb-sized holes that they excavated around the edges of our camp. I dove unsuccessfully in search of spiny lobsters and conch. I explored crevices in the coral for octopus. I ate reef fish, sometimes without even knowing what species they were.

Then came one day when I had the best morning of my entire trip. Danny and I waded onto a broad flat around mid-morning and found more schools of bonefish than we'd seen yet. Within a couple of hours I had landed and released three of them, including a large one that I stalked in water so shallow that his dorsal fin was sticking up in the air. Yet all the while I was thinking ahead to catching dinner. I watched the sun shift overhead, waiting impatiently for the visibility on the flat to wane enough so that I was no longer obligated to chase bonefish. I wanted to get down to something more visceral. More real.

When the time finally came, I went back to camp and swapped out some gear. Then I waded back out to the channel where I'd been catching the snappers. I caught a little one and cut a piece of flesh away from its tail. I pierced that with a hook and cast it back out. As I worked the fly along the bottom, I felt a solid jerk on the line and set the hook. I reeled it in as quickly as possible in order to get my hands on it. I was afraid dinner would get away.

When it came to the surface, I was surprised to see that it was a bonefish. I immediately registered a slight bit of disappointment. I was fishing for meat, and now here I was taking hold of a fish that I was supposed to turn back. It then occurred to me that I really couldn't explain anymore why I was supposed to turn it back. What was the difference, really, between this fish and those other fish I'd been eating? I held the bonefish in my hand as I pondered this question, and I was struck suddenly by how arbitrary it all seemed. I couldn't help but imagine myself trying to explain this conundrum to some ancient hunter-gatherer who had been transported from the past into our modern and confused world. What would he make of it all? After looking at the fish a few more moments, I did the only thing that made genuine sense to me. I slipped an index finger beneath the fish's gill and then walked back to our camp and built a fire of coconut husks. As the fire burned down, I skewered the bonefish's carcass on a stick and wrapped it around with some baling wire so that it didn't fall apart as it cooked. Later, when Danny saw what I'd done, he had nothing at all to say about it. After all, it's hard to talk when your mouth is full of fish bones.

|||||||||||||||||||||||||||||||||||||||||||||||||||||||||||||||||||||||||||||||||||||||||||||||||||||

Tasting Notes: Salmon

There's the old saying that nothing looks better than a ten-day-old tattoo and nothing looks worse than a ten-year-old tattoo. You could say something similar about the taste of salmon, but you're dealing with much shorter time frames. When one of these fish first comes out of the water, there's really nothing that can beat it. When my brothers and I stay at our shack in Alaska, we now and then catch king salmon while we're targeting halibut. We'll take the fish home, still flopping, and slice a fillet into pieces no thicker than a business card. We'll fill a big bowl with an inch of soy sauce and a generous squeeze of tubed wasabi and sit around until there's not a scrap left. While it's sometimes hard to justify the purchase of a cabin that you visit only once or twice a year, one of these meals goes a long way toward an adequate explanation.

Too bad that the taste of fresh fish doesn't last. In fact, you can watch the quality of a freshly caught salmon deteriorate right before your eyes. Flop one into your canoe on a hot, sunny day and it begins to spoil within minutes. At first when you poke a finger into the fish's side, the skin bounces back like it would if you pressed a baby's cheek. Moments later when you do the same thing the skin stays dimpled, as if the fish has somehow become a tad deflated. The eye goes cloudy before you can paddle all the way across the cove. You fillet the salmon out and the flesh is still beautiful, but the suggestion of decay is already haunting you. Suddenly you realize that the black bears you were watching earlier had it figured out: Eat the fish as soon as it's caught, and all the better if it's still in the water.

I feel a little bad for people who have never eaten a salmon within hours of its being caught. More and more, the salmon you get in restaurants is just an approximation of the real thing. A few years ago I was fishing in Chile with my wife and we spent a little time near one of those depressing salmon farms that have proliferated along its remote southern coast. The water inside the nets seemed to simmer from all the activity of the captive Atlantic salmon, especially when the guys came by to scatter loads of pelletized feed. Nearby was a house-sized rock where the sea lions liked to haul out and bask. The rock was stained a weird shade of red. When I asked about it, I was told that the sea lions prey heavily on salmon that escape from the pens. The rock's color was from the artificial dye that is fed to farm-raised salmon in order to give them a natural-looking wild color. Put simply, the sea lions had shit out enough dye to paint a house. I imagined those fish getting distributed around the world, particularly in the United States, and the thought of all those people eating phony trash made me want to either cry or laugh. (Next time you're in a grocery store, you'll notice that farmed salmon actually has an ingredients list.)

Of course, the allure of fake salmon is that you can get it fresh year-round. No waiting for the annual spawning runs, no struggling to preserve large catches for consumption during the long off-season. But in all honesty I'd rather eat rotten salmon that I caught myself in the wild than farm-raised salmon that were reared on dyed cat food in some faraway cage. Not that I'm actually faced with that choice. Over the millennia, humans have come up with all kinds of ways of preserving the annual bounty of salmon in order to hold it over for lean times. My mom used to take the salmon we caught in the Great Lakes region and pressure-seal it in glass Mason jars. Sometimes she'd also put mustard in the jars, or just salt and pepper. The bones would dissolve in the heat. She'd line these jars on the canning shelves in the basement and we'd use the meat to make salmon patties that were mushy and wet but not altogether bad.

My brother Danny, who lives in Alaska, harvests sockeye salmon in the summer from the Kenai, Copper, or Kasilof rivers. He catches the fish with a dip net, and his usual legal allowance is twenty-five salmon for the head of the household and an additional ten fish per each household member. He can fillet salmon faster than anyone I've ever met who's not a commercial fish processor. He eats his fair share of fresh fillets, but a big haul of fish means preserving some as well. You can always try to wrap the fillets and freeze them, but that only leads to disappointment. When you thaw them a few months later, they still look like fresh salmon and you can't help but get your hopes up. Then you cook a fillet and taste it and realize that the fish has already started to turn into something not so delightful. *Rotten* isn't quite the right word. *Skanky* is more like it.

A few years ago, Danny bought a sealer that handles metal cans. He can produce tins of salmon that almost look like something you'd buy from a store—though his tins are a weird army-green color that gives them a sort of postapocalyptic survivalist feel. Other fillets he smokes in a large plywood fish smoker that's powered by a hot plate. Those smoked fillets get vacuum-sealed into plastic bags or else pressure-cooked in glass jars. He does the jarred fish "dry," meaning there's no liquid in there, just glossy, lopsided cubes of smoked fish stacked in a jumble inside a glass jar. He sends a couple to my wife and me every Christmas and we treat them more like decorations than food. I open one only when we have interesting friends for dinner. Invariably they say something along the lines of "What the hell's that?" Shortly after, they say something along the lines of "Damn, that's good."

And I answer: "You should taste one of those things when it's still flopping."

CHAPTER EIGHT

Freeze-up

★

THE MISSOURI BREAKS region of north-central Montana takes its name from the way that the Great Plains break away and crumble into the deep chasm of the Missouri River's canyon. For anyone who yearns for a vestigial hunk of the American frontier, this is the place to find it. Man's efforts to tame the Breaks have been thwarted by rugged geography, a nasty climate, and a suite of uncooperative inhabitants that has included Blackfeet warriors, grizzly bears, and unrepentant horse thieves. It's a huge and wild place, full of animals, fairly empty of people, and abounding in hazards that can put the visitor into lamentable positions of a distinctly western variety.

It's impossible to list them all. For instance, my brother Matt was once bow hunting for elk in the Breaks when he scared up a rattlesnake that zipped toward its hole. Matt caught the snake by the tail just as it went underground. Thinking he'd eat the snake for dinner, he tugged on its tail to pull it back out. When the snake broke in half, its severed body disgorged a couple of baby rattlesnakes that started coming after him and trying to bite him. That's a horrific little story, I know, but it's meant to illustrate my point that someone could spend a lot of time listing the hazards of the Breaks and they still might not think to include the risk posed by preemie rattlers.

But on one particular November morning, while canoeing

through the Breaks in search of mule deer, the direst hazard presented by the landscape was something that almost anyone could have foreseen: The Missouri River was freezing over. From inside my tent I could hear the loud slushy noise of disk ice sliding and bumping along in the current. The trouble with this ice was that it could prevent the downstream progress of our canoes, and downstream progress was just the thing we needed in order to reach the truck that was waiting about thirty-five miles away—the same truck that provided us with the only feasible way of getting us and our gear out of the wilderness.

Matt was lying next to me in the tent. When I asked if he was awake, he said he'd been awake and worrying about the sound of that ice for an hour. It was the same sound that had greeted us in the same tent a year earlier, when our initial attempt to float this stretch of the Breaks ended in failure. Logic might have told us to make our second attempt earlier in the fall, before the arrival of severe cold. But our timing was meant to coincide with the peak of the mule deer rut, when bucks come out of hiding in order to chase does. It's a time of year when you can see deer that you'd otherwise never get a glimpse of, and it's also a time of year when you don't see many people—if you see any at all.

We pulled on our boots and climbed out into the predawn darkness. Each bank of the river was frozen solid for a distance of about twenty feet. Between the frozen edges flowed a matrix of slush and Frisbee-sized hunks of ice that swirled and twirled in the current. Our two companions, my friend Matt Moisan and a guy named Derrick, got out of their tent to check on the situation. Moisan, a lifelong hunter and native Oregonian, offered his assessment.

"That sucks," he said.

Derrick was just a friend of a friend that we'd brought along because we needed a fourth paddler. None of us really knew him, and we didn't care too much what he thought, but he offered his opinion anyway.

"Yeah," he said, "that does suck."

The four of us turned around to look at the land behind us. We were camped in a grove of cottonwoods along an outside bend in the river. Beyond the grove was a broad wedge-shaped flat of land covered in sagebrush, yucca, and prickly pear cactus. The point of the wedge emerged at the terminus of a deep tributary canyon that opened out toward the Missouri through an otherwise impenetrable cliff of sandstone showing a black horizontal band of exposed coal. The canyon itself was narrow and snaky and terminated just a mile or so back, and therefore did not provide a route out.

When I'm not hunting, I always think that I like hunting because it puts you into risky situations that make you feel especially alive. But when I am hunting, I'm tempted to dislike hunting for the exact same reasons. Considering everything, it seemed that the best approach would be to continue downriver in the canoes. After all, we figured, it would be pretty hard to get ourselves into a worse situation than we were already in. We broke our camp and piled the gear into the canoes. There was little sense in paddling, because it was nearly impossible to maneuver in the layer of ice. Instead we joined the flowing mass and let it take the canoes where it wanted. With little else to do, we picked up our binoculars and began scanning for deer. If we were going to get stuck out here, we'd need something to eat.

I might say that fate delivered me to the Missouri Breaks, but it would be just as accurate to say that I was delivered by *Jeremiah Johnson*, the 1972 mountain man flick starring Robert Redford. I first saw the film when I was twelve years old. It tells the melancholy tale of a disillusioned veteran of the Mexican-American War who heads into the Rockies in the 1840s to escape civilization and make his living as a hunter and trapper. He blunders his way through a series of misadventures and unlikely friendships, eventually becoming a feared and respected enemy of the Crow tribe as well as a seasoned hunter. It's the sort of movie that inspires fans to share their favorite quotes. Typical choices include "It is a good rifle, and kilt the bear that kilt me," "Elk don't know how many feet a horse has," and "A woman's breast is the hardest rock the Almighty ever made, and I can find no sign on it."

As good as those lines happen to be, I took greater interest in two slightly more obscure quotes. One comes from Bear Claw Chris Lapp, an aging and obsessive hunter of grizzly bears who takes the starving and bewildered Johnson under his wing to teach him the ways of the mountains. "You can cut wood and leave it up on the Judith; riverboat captains will leave you gold if you put out a pouch. Good to know, if times get hard." The second comes from Johnson himself as he's finishing construction on a crude but gorgeous cabin. A red-tailed hawk flies high overhead, and he looks up to it and says, "He'll be to the Musselshell in . . . Hell, he's there already."

While I recognize that neither of these quotes is likely to end up on a T-shirt, each of them was helpful to me in locating the precise position of what my hyperromantic adolescent brain recognized to be paradise. As everybody knew, hunters were supposed to head west—in fact we *existed* for the purpose of heading west—and I was glad that Jeremiah Johnson had taken the time to offer hints about where I should go. I scoured atlas indexes in the school library looking for the names Musselshell and Judith in order to determine where the action of the movie was meant to take place. I eventually found that both of them were Missouri River tributaries in a region known as the Missouri Breaks.

Once I'd identified the wildest corner of the Wild West, the idea of it bounced around in my head like a fly that's trapped in your car. While my daydreams kept it from totally dying, countless realities— I was too young to move; I'd miss my mom; I didn't have any money; I really ought to go to college; I'd never known anyone who'd actually moved that far away—prevented it from totally living. In fact, the notion existed in a sort of limbo until the summer of 1996, when I had just one semester of college left. Figuring that the anvil of adulthood would soon be crushing down on me, I bought an airplane ticket to Washington state in order to at least get a glimpse of the promised land. At the time, Danny was working a short-term job for the Army Corps of Engineers on a salmon restoration project along the Snake River.*

He took a break from his work and drove over to pick me up at the airport in Spokane. Then, on my urging, we began to pick our way east into Montana. We drove all over the place on confused routes, following streams and rivers and camping on little turnouts where we could fish for trout and cook our meals over fires. One morning I chased after a cow moose and her calves in order to see how close I could get, a practice that I later learned to be one of the stupidest things a person can do in the woods. The next morning I caught my first cutthroat trout and marveled at the bloodred slash on its throat. The beauty of something so aptly named caused me to stop and just

---

*The Snake River is the largest and longest tributary of the Columbia River, which is the largest North American river that flows into the Pacific Ocean. Prior to European contact, the river system supported a salmon run that was inestimably huge, perhaps many times larger than that of any other river south of Canada. Nowadays, thanks to hydroelectric dams and agricultural irrigation and logging and all the other things that make modern American life possible, the Columbia drainage is struggling to maintain any kind of salmon run at all. Danny's job involved a plan to net the salmon hatchlings from the river above the dam and then move them by barge toward the safety of the ocean. There the fish could grow fat and then come struggling back upriver as adults someday in a statistically improbable effort to return to their own natal streams above the dam.

watch the water flow by. Later, as we drove into the Sapphire Mountains, a cinnamon-colored black bear crossed a dirt road in front of us and gave me a look that expressed extreme disinterest in my well-being. It seemed like a taunt, daring me to share its home.

I couldn't help but marvel at the extent of it all: the rolling mountains; the patches of snow still lingering in the shadowed corners of the high country; the jagged peaks across a large valley to the west; the rocky streams; the vast tracts of dead trees killed by lightning-sparked forest fires. At the time I didn't know how to find what I needed in those mountains. I didn't know where to look for elk, where to look for mushrooms, where to find bears in the first few days after they emerge from hibernation. But I didn't need to know those deep mysteries in order to comprehend that they existed. Driving around the West, I was like an illiterate man staring into a book; he doesn't understand what exactly he's seeing, but he damn sure knows it's important.

Back in Michigan, I swapped my buddy Ronny Boehme a Husqvarna chain saw for a burgundy-colored '97 Ford van. I outfitted the van with a Coleman stove and built a bed in the back. Beneath the bed I built a place to stash an ancient Remington .30–06 that I'd gotten from my dad and a twelve-gauge shotgun that had been handed down from my mother's father.

I headed west across the UP and then across northern Wisconsin and Minnesota. Somewhere west of Fargo, North Dakota, I entered what I recognized to be the Great Plains. Shortly after passing into Montana, my route assumed the course of the Yellowstone River. I was now backtracking the 1806 route of William Clark, of the Lewis and Clark expedition, who was probably the first white man to ever travel that river. I passed a place where Clark's men had a hard time sleeping because the buffalo were so loud. An hour or so after that, I passed a place where three would-be settlers are buried beneath a rock pile just off the median of the highway; they disregarded the advice of their guide, Jim Bridger, and took leave of his party in order to take a shortcut through Sioux country. Big mistake. After I drove through Bozeman Pass, the same route that Clark used to reach the Yellowstone, I contemplated taking a room in the Lewis and Clark Hotel. Early the next morning, I followed the Gallatin River downstream to where it meets the Madison and Jefferson rivers to form the Missouri. If I'd jumped into the water there and headed downstream, I'd eventually pass the mouth of the Judith River, where Bear Claw Chris Lapp said riverboat captains would leave you gold if you chopped wood and put out a pouch. The captains used the wood to fuel the steam engines that drove the paddle wheels on their boats. They'd pay a woodcutter, or a woodhawk, about eight dollars a cord. It was good money but woodhawks didn't always enjoy long careers. In the summer of 1868 alone, seven woodhawks were tortured and killed by Indians along the river's course.

Today the mouth of the Judith is known as Judith Landing. We launched our canoes there on our first ill-fated attempt to float this stretch. That time we barely made it into the heart of the Breaks before the river froze over. When it did, we pulled our canoes into a place sometimes known as Cable Crossing. A winding old dirt road met the river there, and we camped on the road's surface where it dead-ended at the water's edge. We stayed there a couple of days, in hopes that the river would thaw or that a truck would come along to rescue us. But soon it was clear that it wasn't going to get any warmer and that no trucks were likely to come along. One morning Matt got up well before daylight, packed some food and a sleeping bag, and started hiking. We had hired a guy to move our truck down to our takeout point, which was forty miles away as the crow flies. The town of Winifred was only about a third of that distance, so Matt headed in that direction. When he walked into Winifred's bar, he found that a significant percentage of that town's 156 inhabitants were having a drink. Matt downed a glass of draft beer and then stood up to address his fellow patrons. "Who wants to make some money?" he asked.

That failure was certainly on our minds when we began to conceive of our second attempt. We were motivated by something akin to vengeance as much as anything else. But now here we were, and this trip seemed likely to end in similar fashion. When we weren't struggling to guide our canoes through the flowing ice, we were wrestling them off the rocks and gravel bars that we got shoved into. By mid-morning we reached the point where we'd been forced off the river on our previous attempt. If we'd been smart, we might have pulled into the landing and then drawn straws to see who had to walk. But things were beginning to look slightly hopeful. The sun had come out bright and clear. As the air warmed, the crisp disk ice that had been locked around our canoes began to soften a little and get slushy on the surface. Instead of feeling as though we were locked onto a moving conveyor belt, we were now able to enjoy a certain maneuverability in the river; or at least we could influence the canoes enough to avoid obstacles.

We were also being pulled along by curiosity and adventure, which tend to override caution. The stretch of river below us was widely regarded as the wildest and woolliest stretch of the Breaks. The fact that we'd failed to reach it before only made us more excited about reaching it now. The allure of seeing what's ahead, just for its own sake, cannot be overstated in any discussion about hunting. Anthropologists have always debated the forces that drove nomadic hunters to push themselves around the world. Factors such as starvation and warfare certainly played a role, but many human movements can only be described as curiosity-infused wanderlust. Imagine that you're a hunter moving down the coastlines of Alaska and British Co-lumbia, the first person to ever set foot on that land. You're traveling on dry ground when you come to the edge of a hundreds-of-feet-tall glacier that terminates at the ocean in a sheer cliff that's calving house-sized chunks of ice. You have two options: one, turn back and make your home at the last place along your route that looked like a suitable habitat; or two, build a skin boat, load up your family, and paddle southward, trusting that there's another side to the glacier. For thousands of years, this continent belonged to those people with the tenacity and curiosity to choose option number two.

Our first opportunity to secure game meat presented itself a few miles past Cable Crossing. Moisan and I spotted some Canada geese far ahead on the left bank of an island. The island was only about thirty yards wide, and I figured that if we drifted along the opposite side of it I'd be able to reach them with a shotgun. We hunkered down in the canoe so that our heads were barely poking above the gunwale. With our paddles held in the water, we maneuvered the canoe into a posi-tion where the island was shielding us from the birds' sight. The sound of the slush camouflaged much of our noise. I held the shotgun ready for when I saw a goose's head or the birds began to lift into the air. I had marked the location of the geese next to a thicket of willows, but we passed that thicket without seeing any. Something had obvi-ously gone wrong, so I stood up to get a better view. I saw that the geese had somehow sensed our presence and had swum out into the current on the opposite side of the island from us. Now they were a tad beyond range and just beginning to take flight. I might have knocked one out of the sky by busting a wing bone with a shotgun pellet, but there was too much of a chance that I'd end up with a crippled bird that flew away instead of a crippled bird that dropped.

As I watched the geese, a flash of movement in the thicket of willows caught my eye. Suddenly I saw a mule deer fawn struggle to its feet. It made it only a few steps before it tipped over.

We beached the canoe and found the scabbed and emaciated fawn in a thicket of willows. What had probably happened was obvious: Coyotes had gotten hold of the fawn, and somehow it had escaped into the water and either swam out to this island or was washed down to it. The tracks in the mud suggested that a larger deer, presumably the fawn's mother, had hung around for a while before taking off. You could hardly blame the doe for giving up. The fawn was missing a good-sized bite from its right back leg, and its left leg was mostly hamstrung. I waved Matt's canoe over to the bank and we discussed the situation. It seemed that the best course of action was to put the fawn out of its misery and strip off its measly bit of usable flesh to eat that night. But, legally, one of us would then be obligated to apply his only deer permit to a half-starved fawn that had lost some of its best meat to a coyote. It was one of those situations where civil and moral law collide. And while the anonymity of the backcountry usually allows you to choose moral law, none of us was willing to risk the punishment of having our hunting licenses revoked. So we left the fawn to its painful death.

We continued downstream for a couple more hours and then started looking for a good place to camp ahead of the coming darkness. We eventually passed a cottonwood grove that was sheltered from the wind, with flat ground for sleeping and plenty of firewood scattered about. We beached the canoes just below the grove, then hauled some of our gear up to the campsite. There was still plenty of time for an evening hunt. Matt and Derrick paddled their canoe across the river to hunt the other side. Moisan and I dragged the other canoe away from the river, where it would still be safe if the wind picked up or the river began to rise. We then headed off on foot, up toward a high vantage point where we could see into a branching network of valleys that came in from the north.

The ridges above the valleys were covered in pines and junipers, and we sat down and studied the spaces between the trees with binoculars. When there's a lot of snow on the ground, the brown color of a deer's body stands out. And when there's no snow on the ground, the white of their rump stands out. But when the ground is a mixture of exposed rock and scattered snow, nothing stands out. That makes seeing deer at long distances about twice as hard as normal. Still, we held tight and glassed a lot of country.

Finally, about an hour before dark, we made out six or seven does that were scattered here and there in the timber. We waited and watched as they fed their way out of the trees and toward an open hillside. We figured that a buck must be in the area, and that he'd probably follow them out. We found him just before dark. He came creeping down the hill and then went from doe to doe in order to stick his nose up under their tails. We watched as they trotted along ahead of him, stealing bites of grass whenever he gave them a break. He was way too far away for us to bother chasing him that night, as it would be dark soon. So we marked his location with a few land features, then traveled through the dark toward the river. When we found our camp, we kindled a small fire so that Matt and Derrick could see it from across the river and find us without too much hassle.

Back in the days before steamboats, explorers and fur traders traveled the upper Missouri River in keelboats. These were powered by oars and push-poles, and sometimes by everyone getting out and pulling on ropes. Upstream progress was slow enough that it would take months to ascend the river to its headwaters. Feeding the crew was a constant issue, and much of the responsibility for doing this fell to a guy whose job title was simple and concise: hunter. He'd get up early in the morning and head into the hills, and then parallel the river in search of game. After making a kill, he'd haul the meat down and hang it in a conspicuous location where the crew would see it, or else he'd wait there until the boat caught up.

Sometimes, of course, the hunters never made it back to the river, having been scalped by Indians. Other times they showed up with considerable fright and visible scratches, having found a grizzly. I've always imagined that such a job would have been to my liking, and I thought about that when Moisan and I got up before dawn and left the river in search of venison. Without a doubt, those bygone keelboat hunters had risen from the same patch of cottonwoods where we'd slept and headed uphill in search of the same game.

We had in mind a long, circuitous route that would bring us toward the buck's location from a downwind direction. We scrambled over loose rock and through deep washouts and collected some cactus tines and yucca thorns in our knees and hands. As the daylight came on, Moisan and I began to recognize a ridgeline covered in thick sagebrush and juniper that climbed like a staircase to the slope where the buck had been chasing does. We eased uphill, with me in the lead. I was concentrating on things far ahead, but all of a sudden I caught a glimpse of a deer's face not much more than a hundred yards ahead of us. It was a good-sized buck, staring down at us from a cluster of juniper. I motioned to Moisan. He moved alongside me and laid his rifle barrel over a juniper limb. The buck turned slightly, offering a shot, and Moisan punched a bullet through the buck's rib cage. It collapsed right where it had been standing.

We gutted the buck and skinned it, then removed the four legs at the upper joints and sawed off the feet at the wrists. These we hung from juniper limbs to cool while we boned out the ribs, neck, and loins. When we were done, we slipped the meat into cotton pillow-

Matt Moisan's buck in the Missouri River Breaks.

cases that I'd bought for a quarter apiece at Goodwill. All of the meat went into our backpacks, and Moisan strapped the skinned-out skull onto the back of his. From where we were, we'd have to hike the buck over two miles of rugged terrain and then we'd be able to let the canoes take over.

Or that was the plan, at least until we'd paddled downstream to the vicinity of Cow Island. There we rounded a bend and encountered what seemed to be a frozen lake rather than the river we'd been traveling on. The water ahead of us was high and still and capped by an uninterrupted jumble of ice that looked like the broken and frozen surface of an Arctic seascape. We paddled to the edge of the ice and found that it was packed solid, but not so solid that you could climb out and walk on it. We made it over to the bank and pulled our canoes out of the water to have a look downstream. Standing on high ground, we could see that the jumbled ice stretched all the way around the next bend. Derrick agreed to stay with the boats while the rest of us headed downstream to see where the ice ended and the river started up again.

Right away, Moisan plunged through the ice on a slough and dunked in up to his head. We then tried to go around the slough, which brought us to an abandoned old homestead building with a collapsed sod roof and a root cellar. People built these structures in the late 1800s and early 1900s. They tried to farm, but the land would usually turn them out penniless and disillusioned within a few years. It seems that hunters have always found a lot more to like about the Breaks than farmers. I thought of this especially when we flushed a cottontail rabbit out of the home's wreckage—our good fortune springing out of someone else's disaster. I shot it with a .22 pistol that I was toting in the lid of my pack, and then we walked another mile downriver without finding an end to the ice. We returned back upstream, stopping at the wrecked homestead long enough to kill three more cottontails. Back at the canoes, we fried rabbit for dinner and then hunkered into our sleeping bags for the night.

Something strange happened while we slept. The day before, we'd beached our canoes at the point in the river where the open water met the ice. But in the morning that border no longer existed. Everything both downstream from us and upstream from us was now a mass of jumbled ice as far as we could see. What's more, the ice-impounded water had risen considerably through the night. Whereas our boats were high and dry when we pulled them up, the sterns were now floating in slush.

We drank some coffee, and then Matt and Derrick walked back downstream to have another look. They came back with two more dead rabbits and a report that the river was dammed up for at least the next two miles. Even if we portaged the canoes and gear down past the ice dam, wherever that happened to be, launching the boats there would be a reckless move. If the impounded water burst through the dam, it could come down in a deluge that might swamp the boats.

We talked about a number of different options before agreeing on a basic plan. First we searched around and found a good overhang of rock that provided some shelter beneath it. We then laid all our gear out, so we could take stock of what could be left behind and what had to come with us. Moisan's buck would have to come out on our backs, so we boned it out to save on weight and then tossed the cleaned bones into a patch of sagebrush. I put a liberal coating of cooking oil on my shotgun to prevent rust, wrapped it in tent fabric, and stashed it under the overhang. We wrapped up our extra clothes, sleeping pads, cooking gear, shotgun ammo, and various other things in another tent and stashed all that under the overhang as well. We sealed off the cache as best as we could with the canoes, and then camouflaged it with sagebrush and juniper. You wouldn't have known it was there unless you stumbled right into it. We figured it would be fine until spring, if we had to wait that long to get it.

In the frontier days it was common for riverboats that were headed to Fort Benton, some 125 miles upstream, to unload their cargo here at Cow Island and stash it on the land like we did. The same shallow water that allowed for the formation of this ice dam would sometimes prohibit the passage of the boats. Fortuitously, back then, there was a fairly easy route down into the canyon on either side of the river here. In fact it was the best route within a hundred miles in either direction, and you could get horses down to the water to pick up the supplies.

Indians knew about this route, of course, as they'd been using it for hundreds of years to move back and forth from the northern Montana plains to the central and southern Montana plains. In September 1877, a party of several hundred Nez Perce Indians came through here and found fifty tons of supplies parked on the river's

My brothers and me on a later, more pleasant trip through the Missouri Breaks.

north bank. The Indians were at war with the United States at the time, having rebuffed the army's demands to submit themselves to confinement on a reservation. Still, they were polite enough to ask the fourteen men who were guarding the supplies for some of their food. The men offered up one bag of hardtack and one side of pork. A gunfight broke out, after which the Indians helped themselves to whatever they wanted and set fire to the rest. A huge stash of bacon was said to have burned through the night with bright orange flames that could be seen from a great distance.

As my hunting partners and I started uphill along the same path that those Indians had taken on their way down, it was hard to imagine a few hundred people having been here all at once. In fact, it was much easier to imagine that we were the first men to cross this land. From our perspective, we were heading into unknown country. We didn't know where we'd sleep that night. We didn't know when we'd be back. But it didn't really matter to us. We knew that we were hunters, and because we were, we'd always be fine.

III

Tasting Notes: Deer

I've killed dozens of them, and I've eaten the meat from way more than I've killed. These have included deer that were hit by cars and trucks, maimed by fences, killed by coyotes, and shot by other hunters. While I'll admit that I have a slight preference for elk, deer are a close second with regard to overall tastiness and versatility. Deer meat is so lean and can be prepared in so many ways that you can eat it every day without getting sick of it, which isn't something I'd say about raccoon or porcupine.

The amount of meat you get off a deer depends, quite obviously, on how big the deer is. They come in a variety of sizes. A mature whitetail buck from the southern mainland of Florida might top out at 125 pounds, while a mature whitetail buck from northern Alberta can easily weigh more than twice that.* Mule deer, which are native to the American West (generally beyond the hundredth meridian), do not vary in size according to latitude as much as whitetail deer do, but they still vary. A typical mature muley will weigh around two hundred pounds, but some whoppers

---

*Christian Bergmann, a nineteenth-century German biologist, was one of the first guys who noticed that larger species of a genus are generally found in colder climates, and smaller species of that genus are generally found in warmer climates. This became known as Bergmann's rule, though it was later redefined to describe how larger members of a particular *species* are found in colder climates, while smaller members of that species are found in warmer climates. This phenomenon has also been linked to latitude, which is obviously closely related to temperature. Heat retention and dissipation are probable explanations for why it's better to be smaller in hot climates and larger in cold climates. For instance, a three-hundred-pound deer has less surface area per unit of mass than a one-hundred-pound deer; the larger deer is better able to retain heat generated through metabolic processes, and the smaller deer is better able to shed heat. The ways in which animals deal with heat can explain a lot about how they behave and how they're shaped. Pigs do not have sweat glands, hence their proclivity to wallow in mud during hot weather. African elephants have large ears (heat dissipation) though woolly mammoths from the Arctic had very small ears (heat retention).

have been reported to weigh upward of 450 pounds. Females of both species generally weigh a lot less than males—usually around one-half to two-thirds as much. Regardless of their size, deer in good condition yield roughly 40 percent of their body weight in boneless meat.

I've only killed one deer that was inedible, and that was hardly the deer's fault. It was a mule deer buck, and the circumstances of its death were so bizarre that it warrants a little explanation. I was hunting the rough country of the Missouri Breaks, in an area with a lot of sinkholes. Most of these holes are found at the heads of steep canyons, where eroded sediments accumulate in thick, loose layers and are then undermined by subsurface runoff. The mouths of the holes are sometimes camouflaged by thick stands of sagebrush. Whenever I find one, I look into the hole to see if there are any old skeletons at the bottom from animals that have fallen in and died of thirst or hunger. A lot of the sinkholes are so deep you can't even see the bottom.

One evening I shot a buck, which slid down an icy slope and dropped from view behind an intervening ridge. When I climbed over to where it had fallen I couldn't find any trace of it. I scaled the hill back to where it had been standing and then followed the trail of smeared blood back downhill. Eventually I traced the deer to the mouth of a sinkhole that was shaped like an Erlenmeyer flask. The hole was about three feet across at the top, about six feet across at the bottom, and about eleven feet deep. I could barely make out details of the buck at the bottom of the hole, though I could see that the animal was still moving a bit. I leaned into the hole and fired a shot down at what I figured to be its rib cage. I didn't see or hear any movement after that, but my ears were ringing horribly because the noise of the rifle blast had bounced out of the hole as if it had been touched off next to my head.

There was no way for me to go after the deer without a rope and some help, so I made my way back toward camp. In the morning my hunting buddy held my ankles while I dangled into the hole and got a lasso around one of the buck's antlers. We dragged the deer out and saw that it was an incredibly old animal. Its muzzle was gray, its back was swayed, its muscles were thin. When we gutted it, we found that its innards had begun to sour. It had been a cold night, but no doubt the insulating effect of the hole had kept the deer from cooling. Still, we scrubbed its abdominal cavity with handfuls of snow. The meat still had a slightly rotten smell to it, but that didn't stop me from bringing it back to the trailer park where Matt and I were living at the time. In our kitchen we started sampling pieces of that deer. Beginning with the rear hams and working toward the neck, we fried little cubes of the meat in butter in hopes that we'd find some cuts that weren't tainted. When the smell of the cooking rot got so bad that we couldn't stand it, we turned on a fan in the back bedroom and began tasting the pieces back there. But there was nothing we could do to salvage it. The sickness in my stomach came from my repulsion from the smell of the meat and also my repulsion over the waste. We placed the deer's meat near a brushy creek bed across the road, not far from where we'd gathered a lot of morels the previous spring. Then we watched as magpies made quick and happy work of what we weren't tough enough to manage ourselves.

People will often use the word *gamey* when discussing deer meat, though I don't think gaminess is in any way synonymous with rot. In the old days, hunters hung venison until it was "high," a term that implied a fairly advanced state of decomposition. But that process was really not much different from the modern practice of aging beef: You hang it until it develops flavor and becomes tender, but you do so under controlled circumstances (in other words, not in a sinkhole with the animal's guts still in it). I've heard people use the word *gamey* to describe meat that might otherwise be described as "off," or "weird," or just plain "bad": bear meat that tastes like fish, beaver meat that tastes like perfume, turtle meat that tastes like some long-dead sea creature that was dragged up from the bottom of a hot swamp, and duck that tastes like . . . well, ducks.

If I had my way, we'd use the word *gamey* only to describe the distinctive pungent glandular taste that comes from certain deer at certain times of year. This sort of gaminess is most common among bucks. You can literally see it on them during the rut, or breeding season, when they foster on the insides of their back legs a mixture of urine along with a secretion from their subcutaneous tarsal gland. The gland is covered by a palm-sized patch of hair that looks like a cowlick with a bad case of bedhead; the oily substance the gland secretes dyes the hair the color of dark honey. It smells so bad that people will pull away and gag if you unsuspectingly put it in front of their nose. You might create a similar odor by pissing on your gym clothes and leaving them in a plastic bag out in the sun.

It would be impossible to calculate just how many millions of pounds of meat have been corrupted by hunters who get that substance all over their hands and knives while processing deer. It took me a long time to make the correlation between tarsal glands and gamey-tasting meat. Finally I read an incriminating passage about the glands in an essay written by Thomas McGuane.* I was soon a believer. When I first explained this theory to Matt, while cutting away the glands from a mule deer buck that we were about to skin and butcher, he was incredulous. Matt picked up one of the glands and put it into the pocket of his backpack. He promised to swab the gland on a beefsteak to see if the resulting taste matched the mysterious and off-putting flavor that sometimes taints his venison. As far as I know, his curiosity wasn't so great that he actually tried it.

Not that tarsal glands are solely to blame for gamey deer meat. A similar flavor can also come from the hard and waxy fat that lies beneath the deer's skin and sometimes between muscle groups. If this stuff isn't

---

*In that same essay, "The Heart of the Game," McGuane relates a conversation in which an anti-hunter challenges a deer hunter. It's one of my favorite pieces of writing of all time. "Why should [deer] die for you? Would you die for deer?" the anti-hunter asks. "If it came to that," the hunter replies.

trimmed away from a deer steak, you might notice that one out of every three or four bites has something gamey going on. If it isn't trimmed away from ground meat used for sausages and burgers, you'll find that it spreads around and affects the entire batch.

I've said so much here about gamey deer meat that I've threatened to undermine my earlier assertion that deer are one of the best-tasting things in the woods. Thinking of this, I'm reminded of that quote by Dr. Martin Luther King, Jr., about how there can be no deep disappointment where there is not deep love. Which is to say, deer meat is usually absolutely delicious—sweet, perfectly textured, like a sublime combination of lean beef and mild lamb—and it's painful when something like a tarsal gland or a hunk of tallow interferes with your ability to enjoy it.

||||||||||||||||||||||||||||||||||||||||||||||||||||||||||||||||||||||||||||||||||||||||||||||||||||||

CHAPTER NINE

The Head on My Shelf

★

THE BUSH PILOT dropped my brothers and me on a gravel bar where a stream that I'll call Nowhere Creek flows into the much larger and glacially fed Forgotten River. This was in the Alaska Range, about 120 miles west of Mount McKinley and 30 miles from the nearest road. It was hot, with daytime highs in the eighties and nighttime lows only down into the fifties. Such weather is rare at that latitude and elevation in mid-August; usually you can expect snow squalls and freezing rain by then. But the surrounding skies were cloud-free, except for the haze of smoke created by wildfires burning in the taiga forest that stretched away beyond the glaciated mountains to the north—fires that wouldn't be put out until the snow started to fly.

We walked off the gravel bar toward a line of spruce trees that began where the floor of the valley tipped upward and climbed toward the mountains. Danny tied a length of parachute cord to a rock and tossed the rock over a high limb. We then used it to hoist up some emergency food and dry clothes and an extra tent where they would be safe from bears. If we got back to the landing strip and the pilot never showed, or if some other kind of disaster struck, then at least we had some supplies to keep us comfortable and fed. We then lifted our packs and started walking uphill. Somewhere up there, we hoped to find Dall sheep.

Our plan was to leave the main valley and follow Nowhere Creek all the way up into the treeless alpine zone. In order to pick up the creek's course we had to navigate a maze of beaver ponds that were bisected by low, grass-covered beaver dams. Along the edge of a pond we kicked up a sharp-tail grouse. It flew a short ways and landed in a spruce tree. Matt shot it for dinner with a load of bird shot fired from a .44 Magnum revolver. He gutted the grouse and stuffed it into the water bottle pocket on the side of his backpack.

As soon as we started following Nowhere Creek we realized that it cut up through a tight canyon full of waterfalls. We then had to leave its course and veer to the right. This move landed us in an alder-choked hellhole with nasty under- and over-layers of downed trees. The alders made it feel like an army of little kids was pulling on our clothes and backpacks, and the downed timber made it feel like we were running an obstacle course of limbo bars and split-rail fences. Eventually we lucked into a moose trail that was beaten into the ground as heavily as a maintained path in a state park. The trail climbed upward and upward, until we finally reached the end of the timber and passed into the alpine zone at a point that was three miles from Forgotten River and two thousand feet higher. The transition was sudden and dramatic, like walking out of a crowded midday matinee into an empty sunlit street.

Here, above the maximum elevation of the spruce trees, the only vegetation that even reached our knees was the band of willows and alders that lined the floor of the valley. The lower portions of the surrounding hills were covered in mixed swaths of gray and brown and green—the gray from exposed outcrops and scree slides, the green from blueberry bushes and crowberry, the brown from dried lichen and sedges and grasses. Up higher, the vegetation gave way to exposed rock that rose up to sharp ridgelines and cliff faces. To the north, toward the head of the valley, the land climbed to a series of

glacier-capped mountains that reminded me of the top of lemon me-
ringue pie.

We slowed our pace and covered just a mile or so of ground before
reaching a flat patch of land that was big enough to sleep three people.
It was so hot that I'd already cut away the sleeves of my T-shirt, so I
dipped the scraps of cotton into a rivulet of springwater that was
seeping from beneath a rock and used them to wipe away the layer of
sweat and pollen that had collected on my face and arms. There was
no need for a sleeping bag in this heat, but I laid mine out anyway for
a little extra padding between me and the ground. We put some water
over an alcohol stove and boiled the sliced-up meat of the grouse.
Then we strained out the cooked meat and used the water to reconsti-
tute a few freeze-dried backpacking meals that we improved by adding the bird's meat. Afterward, we shared a big glob of cheddar cheese
that had melted into a sweaty and bulbous mass inside my pack.

Between eating and falling asleep, we discussed the fact that we
really shouldn't have been hunting in this kind of heat. People always
ask if I lose game meat to bears and wolves, but warmth is a far greater
threat. It will silently ruin meat without a lick of romance while you
are sitting around fantasizing about the threat of predators. But while
it might have made sense to wait for the heat wave to pass, a Dall
sheep hunt is not something that you can simply postpone until another day. We had secured our dates with the bush pilot ten months
earlier by putting down a nonrefundable twelve-hundred-dollar deposit on round-trip flights that would take us into the mountains.
And since reliable Alaskan bush pilots are insanely busy during the
months of August and September, it's quite possible that you'll miss
your entire trip if you miss your dates.

On top of the fee for the bush pilot, Matt and I had each forked
over about six hundred dollars for plane tickets from Montana to
Anchorage. Upon landing in Anchorage, I had dropped another six

hundred bucks for a nonresident hunting license and a sheep tag. When you factor in myriad other incidentals—freeze-dried back-packing food, gas for Danny's pickup, miscellaneous bits of gear—I had well over two grand invested in the hunt. And that sum of money hardly guarantees success. Ninety percent of the sheep hunters who head into the mountains of Alaska without a paid professional guide meet with failure. In other words, only 10 percent of nonguided sheep hunters like my brothers and me get a sheep. Considering that mature Dall sheep rams weigh around two hundred pounds and yield maybe about 35 percent of their body weight in boneless meat, you see that we were faced with a best-case scenario of securing seventy-five pounds of game meat at a price of around thirty dollars a pound. And also considering that there was an outside chance of losing the meat due to factors including but not limited to the heat, you'll see that this venture of ours could hardly be justified as an exercise in subsistence-based hunting and gathering. Instead it was an exercise in something much more controversial and difficult to explain—something that makes me cringe just to say it: trophy hunting.

The next morning we couldn't have killed a Dall sheep even if we'd found one, because the season opener was still a day away. Our plan was to continue up the valley while scouting out the land and keeping a constant eye on the surrounding mountains for sheep. The best and most discreet route seemed to be right up the center of the valley, fol-lowing moose trails or walking on the raised gravel eskers that had been laid down by a river that once flowed beneath some bygone gla-cier.

We used our binoculars to dissect the jagged rims of the valley and also the many side canyons and cirques that opened up to our view as we traveled along. Dall sheep are white, so they do stand out pretty easily against the muted colors of a snow-free mountainside. But their whiteness is obviously not a disadvantage. In fact, the animals spend far more days in the snow than they do on bare ground, and even in the absence of snow they often hang around near the ice-strewn peripheries of glaciers and sometimes even on the glaciers themselves—a type of background that can make them nearly invisible. What's more, they have an affinity for lying beneath rocky overhangs or near crevices in cliff faces, where shadows diminish your ability to see them. Meanwhile, it's possible for them to spot you from extraordinary distances. Dall sheep have eyes that are about eight times more powerful than a human's are, and it's possible to scare them away without ever knowing they were there in the first place. It's essential to see the sheep before they see you, which means you need to be looking for sheep at distances that can be measured in miles rather than yards.

And you're not just looking for any old Dall sheep. In most of Alaska you're only allowed to kill a ram, or male, that meets at least one of the following three criteria: 1) at least one of his two horns must be full-curl, which means it must describe a 360-degree circle when viewed from the side; 2) both of his horns must be broomed, or broken on the ends;* or 3) the animal must be at least eight years old, as demonstrated by the presence of at least eight growth rings, or annuli, on the animal's horns.† Basically, what all of this means is that

---

*It seems that some Dall sheep intentionally broom their horns by rubbing them on rocks once the horns grow large enough to impede their peripheral vision. Brooming might also be caused by the horn breaking off in a fight or in a fall.

†Some people think that the legality requirements on Dall sheep are needlessly complicated, but those people are wrong. While it might be easier to just say that a ram has to be eight years old to be legal, that would put an enormous burden on hunters. Counting growth rings at close range is hard enough, let alone at long distances and in poor light. A full-curl rule would be another way to simplify, but that would remove many sheep from the harvest pool because some rams will never reach full-curl no matter how long they live; their horns just don't grow that way. Other rams that could reach full-curl never will, because their horns either break off or they rub them down.

Matt and I argue about directions on a sheep hunt
in the high country of the Alaska Range.

only about 5 or 10 percent of all the Dall sheep in Alaska are legal quarry.

We pushed along through the morning and into midday, walking and glassing. We spotted plenty of critters, except for the ones we were looking for. A pair of beavers worked in a pond on the valley floor. A young bull moose browsed willows on the lower slopes of a distant mountain. A band of caribou cows and calves were bedded on a snowbank that was sheltered from the sun by a high peak. A young grizzly fed on blueberries at the head of a side valley. But no sheep.

By early evening we were about nine miles in from where we'd landed. Here Nowhere Creek forked into two branches that were

------

Together, these criteria are meant to ensure that only mature rams get killed, and they give hunters a number of ways of determining maturity.

separated by a nose-shaped wedge of land that rose into a high, triangle-shaped mountain. The left branch dropped toward the confluence through a series of waterfalls coming off a high plateau. Above the falls, our map showed that the plateau went only a couple of miles before entering a steep-walled canyon and then terminating at a cirque that would probably be impossible to climb out of. The right branch looked as though it went for about six miles before petering out at the foot of a pass.

We dropped our packs at the junction in order to make a quick scout up the left branch. After climbing past the waterfalls we could see a collection of white spots in the shade of an outcropping that interrupted an otherwise smooth ridgeline. They were miles off, but there was only one thing they could be. I started to form the word *sheep* in my mouth but I was cut off by Matt and Danny saying the same thing.

I sat down and studied the band of sheep with my binoculars. There were eight of them. I noticed that three of them were only about half as big as the other five, and each of the little ones was close to a larger one.

"Looks like ewes," I said.

"That's what I'm thinking," said Danny. "Ewes and lambs."

"You sure there aren't any rams mixed in there?" I asked.

"Not at this time of year. They won't start breeding for another few months, so they'll be separate now."

We kept going. For a while we followed the course of the creek, sometimes walking from rock to rock over the water's surface. But then the land rose up on either side of the creek, threatening to block our view of the surrounding country. We climbed the right bank and angled upward until the creek was just a fine line of white below us. Away from the water the temperature was at least fifteen degrees hotter, and I wiped the sweat from my eyes with the belly of my shirt. We climbed higher and soon hit a trail that was loaded with moose tracks. It continued upstream without gaining or losing elevation, and soon the creek had risen to a point where we were once again level with it. We veered back left to the water and refilled our water bottles, then followed the creek into the mouth of the canyon. It was cool and shaded inside. We went around a couple of bends and now the trail was littered with the bleached bones of a caribou; except for the teeth, the animal's skull had been crushed by time and decay into fingernail-sized fragments that were pressed into the ground.

I was checking the skull out when Matt hissed the words *holy shit* and *ram*, put his hand on my shoulder, and pulled me down. My eyes went toward where he was looking. High above us was a white face surrounded by a mass of horn. The ram was peeking out over a ledge and looking down; it must have heard something just seconds earlier and stood up. It watched as we backed away, seeming unsure of what we were. When we were out of view, we turned and slipped out of the canyon without saying another word. None of us had gotten a good enough glimpse to tell whether the ram was legal, but we figured that we should try to find it again in the morning and have another look—this time without it seeing us. We walked to where we'd left our gear, and then laid out our sleeping bags on a soft mat of crowberry.

My brothers and I were first introduced to Alaska in 2000, when Danny took a permanent job as a biologist at the University of Alaska at Anchorage. At the time, Matt and I were both living in Montana and killing enough meat to keep us fed all year. Right away, though, we started coming up to Alaska on a regular basis to tap into the hunting and fishing opportunities. Our initial jaunts were tame by Dall sheep standards, but still exciting as hell. We launched canoes into rivers we'd never heard of to fish salmon. We walked into mountains that we'd never seen to hunt moose. We made unguided trips into the Arctic to hunt caribou, an animal that I'd never before laid eyes on. Each year, at the end of whatever trip we made, we'd sit around and fantasize about whatever new thing we were going to try next year.

These discussions usually turned to the subject of Dall sheep. Most people who have hunted them agree that they are North America's most difficult game animal. The terrain that Dall sheep inhabit is remote, rugged, and intimidating. People who dream of hunting them put off doing so for decades, waiting for when they have the time and money, only to find that time and money never come or they're too old when they finally do. What's more, we were in a prime position with regard to legal issues. A nonresident of Alaska cannot hunt Dall sheep (or grizzlies or mountain goats) without a licensed outfitter unless he or she is accompanied by a second-of-kin relative who is a legal resident of the state. Second of kin includes brothers, sisters, spouses, sisters-in-law, sons-in-law, grandmothers, etc. With Danny living there, we were able to launch a do-it-yourself sheep trip that would have cost us ten or twelve thousand dollars apiece if we had to hire an outfitter. So, in the early 2000s, we made our first attempt on Dall sheep.

We picked a drainage in the northern Chugach Range, about 130 miles south of where we were now camped but which we could easily drive to. We parked along the Parks Highway and used an old rubber raft to cross the Matanuska River. We then deflated the raft and hoisted it into a tree (grizzlies have a strange tendency to rip rubber rafts to shreds) and headed up a large drainage that came in from the south. We hiked about ten miles to where the valley ended at a big blue-colored glacier and then followed a tributary stream deeper into the mountains. For seven rainy and miserable days we scoured the land without seeing a single Dall sheep. We'd grossly miscalculated our food rations, and by then we were running so low on food that we were cutting pieces of hard candy in half with the serrated blade of a Leatherman in order to share them. On the eighth day we climbed after a sow black bear while I was feeling so weak from hunger that I could barely move my feet. We shot it from a stone's throw away, tagged it, and then feasted on cubes of meat deep-fried in rendered bear oil.

We packed up the rest of the bear's meat and the hide and started hiking out with thoughts about dry clothes and a good night's sleep. A few miles from the road, we passed an incoming stream where you could look up its valley and see a distant collection of peaks that seemed a world away. We took a break from walking and set up the spotting scope for kicks, just to have a look around. Sure enough, there was the first Dall sheep we'd laid eyes on. The animal was standing up near the crest of a far-off peak, like something that had been put there in order to play a joke on us. I zoomed the lens and stared at the sheep until my eye hurt. We'd heard a trick about how to tell a ram from a ewe at long distances: A ram's horn will curl around and block out the white of its neck, so that from far away it looks like the head has been severed from the body. That's what we were looking at here, though from this distance there was no way in hell to determine if he was legal. We had to get closer—much closer.

We hoisted the remaining bear meat into a tree so that the bears wouldn't cannibalize it and then started climbing. By the time we reached the vicinity of the ram, enough hours had passed that he was gone and we couldn't find him anywhere on the mountain. Completely discouraged, we headed back down toward where the bear meat was hanging in the tree. Along the way we had an argument about our routes. Matt split off in order to descend a particularly dicey cliff, while Danny and I went to look for a game trail. We made it back to the bear meat late that night, but Matt didn't return until early the next morning. We then ate some more meat and hiked our way out toward the rubber raft, the river, and just beyond that, the highway. All the while, I thought about how that ram's horn had blocked out the whiteness of the sheep's neck from miles away. Though I could see none of the details of that horn, I became fixated on the idea of it. Better than any piece of man-made art, the horn seemed to encompass all the danger and beauty of a place that would just as happily kill you as let you walk on it. Over the next two years, I watched as Matt and Danny each brought into their homes beautiful heads of Dall sheep they killed on grueling trips that work obligations prevented me from joining. After seeing those horns, I knew I had to have a set for my own home. I remembered reading that Eskimo hunters used to bring home the heads of certain animals and then set them in their lodges in order to treat them as honored guests. I could see where they were coming from.

Now, three years later, we had a rough idea about the location of a ram that might, just might, be legal. We left camp before daylight and found him right at sunup, grazing high on a round-topped mountain that towered above the canyon where we'd found him the day before. The grass and lichens were so sparse up here it looked like he must be feeding on gravel. Whatever he was eating, he'd picked a good spot for himself. There was no obvious way to close the distance on him without spooking him. He could see in every direction, and there was no cover within hundreds of yards. It seemed that the best bet was to get a little closer and then wait for the ram to move into a more approachable position. Since Matt and Danny had already killed sheep on previous trips, we agreed that I'd be the one to make the stalk. Matt would come along with me, while Danny stayed put in order to keep an eye on the sheep in case it moved while we were out of sight.

Two hours later, Matt and I were lying on our bellies within six hundred yards of the ram. All we could see of the animal was its head and neck and the top of its back. We'd gotten this close when it had grazed out of view beyond the crest of the hill, but then it had wandered back and now we were pinned down. If we budged, it would see us for sure. We held tight and whispered back and forth about whether the sheep was legal. Just then I heard a strange and rhythmic clicking noise behind us and turned my head. It was a cow caribou. The noise comes from the way their tendons move over the bones of their feet. She got within spitting distance before she realized we weren't rocks, and then she bucked almost like a wild horse, spun around, and ran off. The movement caught the ram's attention. When I looked back he was staring right at us, stiff-bodied and alarmed. In a blink he turned and ran. I stood up. "Son of a bitch," I said.

All Danny saw from his vantage point was that the ram was headed down toward the canyon. Once it started running, he said, it dropped from his view. "You think it was a legal ram?" he asked.

"Pretty sure," said Matt. "I think his right horn comes full. But we weren't totally sure enough to shoot."

"I can't believe you didn't see him," I said to Danny. "I thought he'd come down right through here."

"He must have been around that bend," said Danny.

We walked up around the bend and the story was clear. A set of downward-running tracks was dug into a hillside of crushed shale so clear and fresh they looked minutes old. The bottom of the canyon was mostly bare rock and wouldn't hold tracks, but we could see the prints where he'd stormed up the other side and disappeared into the cliffs.

It was an impossible-looking slope, and it would be a nasty climb, but we had in our heads a piece of advice that Danny and Matt had gotten from a bush pilot they once hired: "Find the one you want," he said, "and stay with it."* For a lot of animals that advice just wouldn't work, as they can vanish into deep timber and brush. But the open country that allows a sheep to see you from miles away also allows you to see him from miles away. If you spook one and then climb through the same terrain that he does, the pilot explained, there's a good chance that you'll run into him over the next couple of days. We kept this advice in mind as we discussed what we ought to do, though in the back of our heads was the reality that we weren't even sure the ram was legal. Eventually it came down to a vote. Matt and I voted to follow the ram; Danny voted to go look for another one.

We followed. It was a hot and miserable climb, often so steep that we had to dig our fingertips into cracks in the rock to pull ourselves up. There were a few springs trickling out of the rocks, and the mountain was steep enough that you could stand beneath them like a shower.

It took a couple of hours to gain the summit, a square-shaped butte almost as flat as a football field and about that size. The entire surface was scattered in sheep droppings. Some were fresh and some were old. On every side, the land dropped away into sharp descending ridges and jumbles of collapsing rock. We began stalking around the edges, slow and easy, often crawling to the edges on our bellies in

*Funny little story: The same guy that gave us that advice is to thank for us knowing about this spot. One time, Matt and Danny were sitting in the pilot's hangar near the town of Wasilla while they waited for the weather to clear so that this pilot could fly them into the mountains. The pilot was fielding calls from various hunting guides that he worked for, and Matt and Danny overheard a conversation between him and a guide about a specific valley that the guide wanted to visit on horseback because he knew that there were some rams in the area but no hunters. Matt and Danny went home and studied that valley on a map and noticed that there were no landing strips in the vicinity. The only way to get in there was to land on a gravel bar at the mouth of the creek and then bushwhack through a couple thousand vertical feet of nasty terrain. Later Danny asked that pilot if he could fly us in to the gravel bar, and he said he could not because one of his guides sometimes hunted the area. So we called another bush pilot up in Fairbanks instead, and he agreed to drop us in there, no problem.

order to peek over the side and survey the confused terrain below. By moving along, we could steal angled glimpses backward and ahead and see into shadows and crevices that we hadn't been able to see into when we were directly above them. At one point I took off my sunglasses and set them at my side in order to rub my eyes and wipe the sweat from my face. Just then some kind of pipit, a small passerine bird, landed right next to me and started to attack his own reflection in the lenses. I was wondering if he could actually damage the glass when I heard a whisper and saw that Matt was on his belly just a ways down the ledge. He was motioning me forward. I started to get up and he gave me the "stay low" gesture with his hand. I crawled over and he said, "Three rams."

They were bedded in an indentation of the cliff face about three hundred yards below. The one we'd been following was there, along with two other young and nonlegal rams that he'd joined up with. They were straight down enough that I could have thrown a rock and landed it among them. All were staring downhill. While Dall sheep predators—such as wolves, grizzlies, and lynx—are some of the most badass critters in North America, sheep usually trust that they'll be coming from downhill. In fact the sheep seem almost incredulous that some other animal would outclimb them in tough terrain. While this assumption has served the species well over the millennia, right now it was a major oversight. We were able to nestle into the rock and take our time while we again tried to ascertain the legality of the ram.

If the right horn was full-curl, as Matt suspected, it was only barely full-curl. At this angle it was tough to tell for sure. But the position of the sheep, and the fact that it was holding still, made Danny fairly confident that he could count the horn's annuli with the spotting scope. We set the scope on a tripod, moving slowly and quietly, and trained it on the ram's head. For thirty minutes we took turns counting, trying to sort out the annual growth rings from the horn's lesser rings and grooves. To make a mistake is a major deal. If you screw up and kill an illegal ram, you can face heavy fines and even jail time. Of course, you could also walk away and no one would ever know, but you'd have to live with the knowledge and that's as ugly as any fine or penalty.

I was reluctant to make the call, but eventually Danny's hesitation faded. "I'm telling you," he whispered, "that ram has at least eight annuli. It's legal. If I were you, I'd take the shot."

To know Danny is to know that he doesn't screw up. I placed the crosshairs of my rifle behind the sheep's shoulder, then considered the steep angle of the shot and adjusted my point of aim. I took a breath, let half of it out, and squeezed the trigger. The ram stood up, but then he got woozy looking and toppled over and dropped from view.

In spite of the fact that a slip and fall could have been fatal, the three of us half-scrambled and half-slid down the cliff face without even thinking of the danger. Far and away, the most exhilarating moments when you're hunting big game in rough country come as you're climbing up or down toward a fallen animal. It felt as if I might explode with tension and stress and anticipation. And then I finally got down to where I thought the animal would be, but it wasn't there. I was hit by a horrible feeling that the wounded ram had escaped. Matt rushed past me and climbed down to the next ledge and then let out a whoop. There it was, dead.

The horns of a Dall sheep are so bizarrely curled and beautiful, and the first thing I did was lift the ram's head by its horns in order to feel their mass and power. Through the horns, a sheep can deliver and receive blows with about forty times the energy required to fracture a human skull. But the initial thrill of holding the horns was quickly replaced by a panicked feeling. Neither of the horns seemed to come quite full circle. Instead of curling tightly, they spiraled outward in long, lazy arcs. Only one side was broomed, and that one only slightly.

I frantically began counting the annuli, as did Matt and Danny. We counted together from the base outward, and then recounted the rings from the tip back toward the base. Without a doubt, the ram was nine years old. It was legal.

I grew up surrounded by hunting trophies. The heads of wild hogs, deer, and bears decorated the walls of our living room, though *decorated* might not be the best word for all of them. You might just say that these trophy heads defined our walls, and in some cases haunted them. What comes foremost to mind is the head of an eight-point buck that hung on the wall of our living room. My dad shot the buck in Michigan in 1985, while hunting from a tree where a cornfield edged up to a grove of red pines. The arrow entered the buck high on its rib cage and a few inches to the right of the spine, in the area of the back where a human has a hard time scratching himself. The buck then ran off, carrying the arrow with it.

We spent the whole night looking for that deer, and much of the next day, without ever finding a single drop of blood or a helpful set of tracks. My dad knew that the placement of the arrow should have meant a dead deer, but somehow it hadn't. Perhaps the arrowhead had broken apart on impact without doing any damage, or it had lodged into bone without penetrating the deer's vital organs, or some other unknown factor had allowed the deer to survive. We cut wider and wider circles through the woods surrounding the cornfield, but eventually we abandoned the search and gave up. My dad was unusually quiet for days.

A couple of weeks went by, and then Michigan's general firearm season opened. Danny went out to hunt, and on the way to his stand he passed through the cornfield near my dad's tree stand. In the darkness he encountered the deer's body as it lay on its side with the arrow protruding from its back. From there he could look across the tops of the corn and see the canopy of the tree where my dad had been hunting, not thirty corn rows away. Later that night, after visiting the deer's body, we entertained the idea that the buck must have run far away after getting shot and then returned days later to die in that spot. But we quickly admitted that this theory was pure bullshit. The arrow, which had penetrated a lung and then lodged against a rib without exiting, would have dealt death quickly. The deer had been there all along and we simply hadn't found it, either through bad luck or stupidity and poor tracking skills or a lack of diligence. The meat was far gone, spoiled and pecked by birds and scavengers, though my dad removed the deer's cape and antlers and brought them to a taxidermist. And while unknowing visitors to our home might have seen that deer as some childish emblem of conquest, what they were actually seeing was my father's self-inflicted reminder of his own fallibility as a hunter.

Now that this set of sheep's horns had come to me, I knew that they would live with me for the rest of my life as some sort of symbol. Whether that symbol would be good or bad now depended on our ability to salvage the meat in spite of the wickedly hot temperatures. Earlier we'd put that idea out of our minds in order to concentrate on hunting, but now it was coming back around like a boomerang that threatened to knock us in the back of our heads.

The key to handling game meat in the field is to keep it cool, a job that needs to begin right away. A sheep's body temperature is several degrees warmer than a human's, so already the animal was in a dangerously hot state. We quickly gutted and skinned the carcass, then removed all of the meat from the skeleton and laid the pieces out to cool on shaded rocks. Ideally you'd be able to leave it like that for several hours, especially if there's a nice breeze, because that will cause a hard, protective rind to form on the outside. But almost immediately we had a fly problem, so we had to put all the meat into protective mesh game bags to prevent it from getting covered in eggs.

As soon as we were done butchering we had to make our second compromise. We needed to climb back up the cliff before it got dark, which meant packing up the meat before it cooled off. If we put it directly into our backpacks, we knew it would bleed through the mesh game bags and saturate our packs with blood, and then we'd be walking around with grizzly bait strapped to our backs for the rest of the trip. So we had to put the game bags inside a few of the plastic contractor bags that Danny had stuffed into the bottom of his pack, which further hampered the meat's ability to dry and cool.

It seems counterintuitive, but you get into trouble in the mountains by climbing things that you can't get down rather than going down things that you can't get up. It's basically the same problem that young cats get into when they ascend a tree. But this scenario gets turned on its head when it comes to hunting big game. If you drop down a steep face in order to retrieve a large dead animal, getting back up with a large burden can be a serious problem.

Once we loaded all the meat, I strapped my rifle and the skull of the sheep to the outside of my backpack with a length of bungee cord. We then started up the cliff. Two of us would give the first guy a boost up the ledge, and then we'd hand the packs up to him. Then the man on the ledge and one of the guys below would pull and push the second person up. The two guys on the ledge would then grab the third guy and drag him up. It was tough going, but within an hour we'd reached the crest of the ridge from which I'd shot the ram. From there it was just a three-mile downhill walk to where we'd left our sleeping bags about sixteen hours earlier.

———

There was no good place near our camp to hang the meat, so we slept close by in order to be able to hear a grizzly if it got into the meat. By the morning the meat had cooled off nicely, but the mesh game bags had become so saturated with blood that flies were laying their eggs directly on the cloth. Now the outsides of the bags were sprinkled with what might be mistaken for bread crumbs or shredded parmesan. We hauled all the bags to a clean gravel bar and emptied them out on the rocks. Then, while I used willow switches to keep the flies off the meat, Matt and Danny used my little mini-bottle of shampoo to wash all of the game bags in the creek. After rinsing them thoroughly and wringing them dry, we rebagged all of the meat and began building a tightly woven wigwam of willow limbs that would provide shade during the hottest part of the day and hopefully help deter the flies. We were only half done with this when we realized the futility of our plan. The flies had wasted no time rediscovering their egg-laying habitat, and by mid-morning the sun was hot enough to mitigate the cooling effects of the stream. Already we were standing around with no shirts on while we fretted about the situation.

I put forward the idea of hauling the meat uphill to a snowfield. We could dig out a hole in the snow and bury it. The problem with this idea was that the nearest snow was miles away. We kicked around a few more ideas, and finally Danny came up with the idea of double-wrapping the meat in contractor bags and sinking them into the creek.

We placed all of the meat back into the plastic liners, and I used my emergency roll of duct tape to seal the packages. I waded into the creek and found a knee-deep hole that had formed beneath a dense overhang of willows. The water was cold enough to make my bones ache. I reached in and pulled out a bunch of fist-sized rocks in order to expand the hole and make it deeper. Matt then handed in the bags one by one, and I held them in place while Danny anchored them beneath mounds of boulders. With that taken care of, we were free of the burden of having to constantly monitor the meat's exposure to flies and heat. There was still the remaining threat of bears, but that's just something you have to learn to live with or it will drive you crazy.

We repacked our gear and headed up Nowhere Creek into fresh territory. A mile or so up, we struck off along a tributary stream that flowed in from the east. We followed it for a couple of miles, passing some ewes and lambs that watched us without concern from the heights of the overhead cliffs. Later we spooked up two young rams that skittered away. After that we didn't see much of anything, and we worried that we'd run off whatever sheep were in the area. In the evening we came to the head of the drainage and then climbed toward a low pass that would deliver us into a neighboring tributary that flowed back toward Nowhere Creek. When we reached the pass, we could see most of this drainage and it didn't look very interesting. We hung a right instead and followed the ridgeline deeper into the mountains. By then our water bottles were empty, so we walked out along a spur of the ridgeline toward a snowfield where we could gather some snow to melt when we made camp. From there we could see into yet another valley, and at the head of that valley was a scattering of a dozen white specks. Through the spotting scope, two of the specks appeared to have necks that were not connected to their bodies. There was no way to get to the sheep that day, so we laid out our sleeping bags near the snowfield on a narrow flat of land between two cliff faces. The patch of ground was barely big enough to accommodate us, maybe about the size of two barroom pool tables. As we dozed off, Matt said, "If I'm not here in the morning, throw my boots over the ledge and I'll climb up for breakfast."

We began walking at daybreak and soon found that the gang of sheep had stayed put through the night. They were in the head of a valley that was shaped like an amphitheater. The ten ewes and lambs were on one side, the two rams on the other. Both of the rams were big; at least one of them was definitely legal. What was less definite was how we'd ever get close to him. He and the other ram were feeding and milling about in a bowl-shaped meadow at the head of a long, vertical snowfield. The bowl was near the upper lip of the amphitheater; from there the rams could see everything and anything that happened in their vicinity. What was more, it would be equally impossible to sneak past the ewes without alarming them. To put all this in baseball terms, imagine a stadium with a two-mile diameter. Then imagine that the rams were seated in the upper decks of the stadium above third base, with the ewes above second base and us hidden beneath the seats above first base. We couldn't simply walk down and cross the field and then climb up, because the sheep would see us the whole time. So instead we had to climb over the backside of the stadium and descend down toward the parking lot. Then we had to walk around the periphery of the stadium and from the outside judge the exact location of the rams' seats. When that was done, we had to again scale the outside wall of the stadium and climb up and over the edge, hoping to arrive at a spot just above the rams and looking down on them.

It took us eight hours to reach that position. By that point we had no idea if the sheep were still below us. They had had plenty of time to wander off and could have strayed miles away. We were prepared for disappointment when we got down on our bellies, crawled over the lip of the amphitheater, and inched forward. Soon the strip of snow was in view. With that landmark in sight, it was easy to locate the two rams that were still exactly where we'd left them. There was no need to guess about the legality of the big ram; I took one look and said "Legal! Legal!" Danny then dropped the sheep with a single shot. It tipped forward and hit the snow and went sailing downhill like a toboggan. We ran to the snow slide and jumped on, backsides down, and slid after it. I was sliding so fast that I had to dig my heels and elbows into the ground below me in order to slow myself down. After a few hundred yards we still hadn't seen the sheep, but the smeared blood on the snow indicated that it hadn't gotten back to its feet. Finally, a couple of hundred yards downslope, we found the sheep wedged against a rock that had melted up out of the snow.

It was late that night by the time we got the second ram butchered and packed down to where we'd left the first ram stashed beneath the surface of Nowhere Creek. We approached noisily and from upwind, in case a grizzly had gotten into our things. While there was no evidence of bears, flies had certainly been present. I'd left the ram's skull in the shade of a willow without wrapping it up because we needed to save our remaining bags for meat protection. It was crawling with hundreds and hundreds of maggots. I waded out and dunked it into some fast-moving water and scrubbed it with my hands. Most of the maggots were carried downstream as fish food. I then took out my knife and carved away some of the nastier pieces of flesh that were still clinging to the skull.

In the morning we retrieved the meat from the creek and everything looked great. Cool and bug-free. Some of the meat had gotten wet and the water bled it of color, so we trimmed that away and then kindled a small fire with willow limbs to cook some of the meat for breakfast. After eating, we packed everything up for the walk. With the gear and rifles, plus the meat and heads of the two sheep, each of our bags now weighed between ninety and a hundred pounds. A day of walking got us about eight miles down valley. In the afternoon we passed some scattered, windblown trees, and soon we reached the sharp edge of the forest. Below us, Nowhere Creek dropped over the falls and plunged down toward the big glacial river.

The air had finally cooled off and a breeze had picked up, so we unpacked all the meat and laid it on rocks where it could dry out and

Danny and I pack out a pair of Dall rams.

the wind would keep the flies away. We camped near it so we could protect it from bears. The skull from Danny's sheep still smelled fresh, so we laid it on top of the meat. I wrapped mine in my extra shirt to keep the flies off and then walked it downhill and into the timber so I could put it into a tree where it would be safe and we didn't have to smell it.

We got a slow start in the morning, aching and sore from the previous day's pack-out. As we organized our gear for travel, we heard the distant buzz of a plane. It came down valley, passed directly over our heads, and then began a slow circle that would take it toward the gravel bar where it had left us off. We knew the pilot wouldn't wait forever, so we forgot our aches and pains, dumped out our instant coffee, and hurried down into the thick timber. On the way past the tree where I had hung it, I stopped to retrieve the skull. The cool air had done it favors; it was drier now, and smelled less, and the extra shirt had prevented the introduction of more fly eggs. Even in its un-savory condition, it had already become a symbol of the mountains' beauty, of my love for my brothers, of the wildness of the land, of the pain of walking long distances under a heavy load. I fastened it to my pack, using bungee cords to hold it tight against the mile or so of snagging and grabbing alder bushes that waited below us. Once I got the skull the way I wanted it, I glanced downhill and saw that my brothers had nearly vanished into the timber below me. I rose to my feet and followed.

III

Tasting Notes: Camp Meat

Back when my dad was alive, he and his old-timer friends liked to reminisce about making "camp meat." This was code language for the practice of shooting a deer that was additional to whatever amount of deer you were legally allowed to harvest, and using the phrase in casual conversation implied that a cavalier and woodsy strain of lawlessness ran through your blood. As long as the animal was entirely consumed while you and your friends were in camp, and the bones were pitched into a river, there'd be no evidence of the crime once you left the woods and returned home with your legally killed quarry.

Killing an illegal deer for camp meat is more or less a bygone practice nowadays, though plenty of cavalier and woodsy meals still get cooked and eaten by hunters out in the woods. Motivations for these meals can be as practical as being out of food, or as whimsical as wondering what some critter would taste like if you cooked it over a fire. Usually, though, it's a combination of the two: You're out of food, or nearly so, which gets you to wondering . . .

I practiced for these scenarios long before they happened to me in real life. Starting when I was eight, my brothers and I would sometimes paddle our canoe away from our home on Middle Lake and through a channel that led into Twin Lake. We'd camp on an uninhabited island that was so small and so close to shore that a woman once yelled across the water that we needed to watch our language. But even limited removal from civilization seemed like an excuse to eat freshly caught bluegill fillets that were burned to a blackened crisp in an aluminum Boy Scout mess kit set over a ripping fire. Other fires back then cooked other meats, all of them equally unpalatable. A skinned-out English sparrow poked on the end of a stick like a marshmallow and dehydrated over a bed of coals comes to mind. So does a chipmunk that I shot with a .22 while out squirrel hunting with my dad when I was eleven. The animal was about as heavy as a pair of sunglasses and as fatty as a stick of celery. I cooked it on a spit over a fire next to our truck, and the meat came out so tough that my teeth felt kind of loose after I finished trying to pull it away from the bone.

Regardless of taste, those meals made me fantasize about getting into situations where I'd have to prepare camp meat in real life. Such situations finally began to materialize once I moved out West and started hunting remote country, where you need to carry your provisions on your back. Matt and I would pack into the mountains on four- or five-day hunts, sometimes longer. We'd skimp on our supply of food in order to cut down on pack weight. Then, after a few long days of eating little besides freeze-dried food and tortillas wrapped around blocks of cheddar cheese, we'd start to regret our judiciousness. By then the sight of a spruce grouse was enough to make our mouths water. We'd shoot the birds with arrows and then cook the meat over a fire. It always turned out bland when boiled, if not a touch piney. Clearly, roasting was the way to go. But that method had its own problems. When subjected to heat, the legs and wings of the birds splayed out in a spread-eagle fashion and always got completely dried out and overcooked by the time the breast meat was safe to eat.

At some point, we started packing for certain hunting and fishing trips with the assumption that we'd secure food along the way. With this assumption came a desire on my part to learn how to handle what I considered to be the trifecta of common but difficult-to-cook camp meats: fish, game birds, and small mammals. (I don't mention big game here because it's almost too easy: just skewer kabob-sized pieces and cook them like hot dogs over a fire; it can't be messed up.) Each type of creature presented its own set of problems, but I conquered those problems through gung-ho resourcefulness and a lot of tinkering. I hit on a memorable way of cooking fish while on a caribou hunt in the Arctic. When my friends and I tired of grayling and char fillets fried in a pan of sooty bacon grease, I tried breading them in Pringles potato chips that I pulverized between two rocks. They were sublime, though I admit that that recipe was like a culinary form of cheating. The first time I ever made a legitimately restaurant-worthy meal of camp meat was on a float trip in Alaska. We were catching coho salmon that were so fat you couldn't grill them over a fire because they'd drip and burn, as if they were coated in lighter fluid. So we made fish baskets from willow limbs and roasted the fillets propped off to the side of the flames, the way they cook whole lambs in Argentina. In the Rockies, I learned of the perfect way to cook freshly caught trout over a fire without the use of anything but a knife. First gut the trout and pull out the gills, but leave the heads on. Then run the sharpened end of a skewer into the fish's mouth and poke it into the flesh at the back end of the abdominal cavity. To keep the fish from falling off the skewer, whittle some sticks of green wood about as thick as the thin end of a chopstick and as long as your finger. Poke three or four of these perpendicular through the fish's body, so that the skewer is wedged between them and the fish's spine. It ought to look like this:

I got my first valuable insight into cooking small mammals when I was hanging around in Vietnam with my wife and my brother Danny. One day, we cruised up into the mountains outside of Nha Trang on rented mopeds. We were headed to a waterfall where you can jump off some cliffs into a plunge pool, but on the way we passed a small family farm that had a pile of coconuts and a bundle of sugarcane sitting next to a sugarcane crusher out by the dirt road. This was an advertisement for a refreshing drink that they make there with those two ingredients. While we sipped our drinks, I noticed a freshly dead critter lying on a log next to an outdoor fire. It was about the size and shape of a small opossum, with an opossum's face and the tail of a squirrel. I mimed my interest in that sort of thing to the farmer, a man in his forties who was wearing nothing besides a pair of cutoff shorts. This pleased him greatly. He did an expert job of miming his reply: He'd just shot the thing out of a tree with an air gun, and it had had it coming because the animal kept getting into his corncrib.

The farmer tossed the entire thing, complete with the head, guts, and tail, into the embers of his fire. He stirred the marsupial around and around with a stick. Soon the hair was completely scorched away, yet the skin was still intact except for a few charred places around the knees, toes, and lips. The farmer took his machete and scraped away the ash and then gutted the animal. From the small pile of guts he removed the kidneys, heart, and liver, and put them back into the chest cavity, along with a few leaves and a pepper that he plucked from his garden. He sprinkled the whole thing with a bit of salt and an assortment of dried spices that he pinched from cups made from coconut shells. Then he wrapped the gutted and hairless critter with a few layers of palm leaves that he whacked out of a tree with the machete. He placed the package directly on a bed of coals.

We shared a few rounds of rice wine while we watched the thing cook. After about an hour, just as the leaves were beginning to smolder and burn through, he removed the package from the fire and peeled away the leaves. Using his machete and a block of wood, he split the animal down the spine and then chopped those halves into many small pieces. I lifted up a chunk that was adjoined to a heat-shriveled foot. The meat pulled away almost effortlessly. I was blown away. Using nothing but the things in his yard, this hunter had created a meal that I couldn't have replicated with all the help of all the grocery stores in America. The meat

The hunter and his kill. Nha Trang, Vietnam.

had the dense flavor of perfectly seasoned squirrel, but with skin as fatty and satisfying as crisp chicken skin.

Months later, I was still describing that meal as the highlight of my trip. It wasn't long before I tried out the method on a squirrel: I singed off the hair and seasoned the meat, then cooked it over the coals inside aluminum foil. (There's a paucity of palm leaves in many parts of America.) It worked perfectly, in that it was tender meat that tasted good. Next I tried it with a rabbit. Also good. Soon I struck on the idea of forgoing the foil and just letting the skin serve the same purpose. But instead of placing the meat directly on the coals, where it could burn, I suspended the squirrel over the embers on a rack of willow limbs. I knew that it was working when I poked the squirrel's skin and the cooking juices squirted out like a squeezed lime. I realized that I was essentially braising the meat with its own liquids inside the container of its own skin; not much different than roasting a whole hog, just a hell of a lot wilder. And therefore, better.

Lastly, I figured out how to cook wild game birds as camp meat. My solution for these came down to patience and, to a lesser extent, trussing. Basically, you truss a bird by wrapping its legs and wings close to its body, so that it forms a tight little package that can be cooked in a uniform way. This is generally done with kitchen string, though in the field I've used strands of barbed wire, pieces of cable wire cut away from frayed and discarded logging chokers, and, in the case of woodcocks and snipe, by using the bird's own beak as a skewer to pin the thick part of their legs to their breastbones.

Once the bird is trussed, you need to suspend it away from the fire's flames but still within range of the fire's heat. You want it close enough so that you can hold your hand next to it for about four or five seconds before you have to pull away. Spits set across two forked sticks that are shoved into the ground are great. So are pieces of wire hung from an overhead limb, especially if the wire is flexible enough that you can bend it in order to change the bird's height and spin it around.

However it's done, the bird has to be cooked very slowly. A fist-sized quail might take twenty-five minutes. A grouse might take forty-five. A duck, an hour. It goes by feel, and the only way to get the feel is by doing it. And if you get impatient while you're at it, remind yourself that you're trying to do something that 99 percent of Americans can't do. After all, if it was easy, you'd already know how.

|||||||||||||||||||||||||||||||||||||||||||||||||||||||||||||||||||||||||||||||||||||||||||||||||||||||

CHAPTER TEN

Killing Proper

★

THERE IS A right way and a wrong way to kill a wild animal, and I don't mean that in a practical sense. An explanation of this is tricky, similar to explaining why it's more pleasurable to spend money earned through hard work than money earned through dubious means. It comes down to metaphysical issues, things of the heart. I was thinking about this one day while I was hunting mountain lions with a pack of about a dozen dogs in southeastern Arizona. They were tall, lanky hounds—most with Walker bloodlines—owned by my companions Floyd Green and Joe Mitchell, two well-known mountain lion* hunters with a combined lion-hunting experience spanning about sixty years and five hundred cats. Many of their dogs showed physical evidence of past skirmishes with lions, including slit ears, lacerated noses, and scarred muzzles. The injuries were usually suffered when they brought a lion "to bay," a term for when hounds chase their quarry into a tree, or corner it against a cliff, or trap it in a cave, and then hold it there until their master shows up to deal with the beast. Earlier I had mentioned to Floyd that it seemed as though a

---

*Other common names for this species (*Felis concolor*) include catamount, cougar, painter, panther, and puma; there are a bunch more esoteric ones.

dog would lose his taste for hunting lions once he got scratched a time or two. "It's the opposite of what you'd think," replied Floyd. "It just makes 'em hungrier."

I was camped with Floyd and Joe at an old abandoned ranch house not far from Aravaipa Canyon, at the end of a driveway that takes more than an hour to travel. Along this route, on our way in, we saw where something had been dragged across the road from west to east and then down into a dry arroyo. At the end of the drag marks was a dead buck with picked-clean bones that had been buried with leaves and dirt beneath a scrubby little oak. The hide was in pieces but still connected to the carcass here and there, like a person who passed out drunk in bed without getting completely free of his clothes. Floyd tipped his cowboy hat and peeled back the deer's skin to show me the blood clots and teeth marks around the animal's neck. He also showed me where the spine had been wrung around in circles three or four times. There wasn't a doubt in his mind that we were looking at a lion kill, though it was at least a week old. This was good news. We'd come to hunt this area because a local rancher had lost fifty calves to lions here the previous spring—about nine months earlier—and this was proof that at least one lion was still hanging around.

If you had asked me ten years earlier, I would have told you that I'd never want to hunt a mountain lion. "What's the challenge," I would have asked, "in shooting a cat out of a tree?" The notion of challenge is one of the most hotly debated aspects of hunting. Definitions of the word evolve so constantly, and are so subjective, that it's hard to find two hunters who define it the same way. As a way of dealing with the confusion, some of us abide by a more readily definable synonym known as *fair chase*. It's an ethical term that provides hunt-

ers with a guiding principle to abide by. Jim Posewitz, the founder of
Orion the Hunter's Institute, writes that fair chase "addresses the
balance between the hunter and the hunted. It is a balance that allows hunters to occasionally succeed while animals generally avoid
being taken."

Some hunting strategies are such an affront to the idea of fair
chase that hunters share an almost universal disdain for them. For
example, most hunters would agree that dynamite shouldn't be used
for duck hunting because it would take away the challenge. Most
hunters would also agree that night-vision goggles shouldn't be used
in deer hunting, for the same reason. Often, as is the case with these
examples, our notions of fair chase are enforced by law. It's illegal to
kill ducks with dynamite. It's also illegal to hunt deer with the aid of
artificial lights.

However, fair chase is not universally legislated. Certain activities
that are definitely not fair chase, such as the pathetic practice of hunting animals inside high-wire fences, is permissible in many regions as
long as it's done on private property and with the proper legal per-
mits. Whether or not a hunter chooses to participate in this limp-
dicked activity comes down to personal choice. Other issues of
personal choice are much more nuanced than the above example,
though they're taken no less seriously by many sportsmen. Over the
years I've met hunters who eschew rifles with telescopic scopes because they prefer the challenge of using rifles with open, or iron sights.
I've met hunters who don't use rifles because they favor the additional
challenge presented by compound bows. And I've met hunters who
gave up on compound bows in order to take on the even more difficult challenge of hunting with a handmade longbow. However, some
hunters who use handmade longbows hunt deer by sitting in a tree
stand next to a bait pile, a practice that is considered unchallenging by

many guys who prefer hunting on foot in open country with a rifle and a telescopic scope.*

I generally believe these differentiations to be positive, however nitpicky, because they demonstrate that hunters are thinking people who struggle to define the limits of their world. I know that I certainly do, though I've come to realize that rigid boundaries are sometimes hard to determine. Consider something that happened to me while I was living for about nine months along the Bighorn River in Wyoming. While there, I became friends with a hay farmer whom we'll call Bill. He had a side business raising game birds. He would buy pheasant and chukar hatchlings from a wholesaler for around a dollar apiece and then raise the birds to maturity inside huge tentlike structures made of netting. Hawks and falcons would dive at the birds from above and hit the netting so hard that they'd blast through like it was wet newsprint, so the upper portions were reinforced with wire fencing. Bill fitted each bird with a little piece of plastic called a blinder, which worked much like the blinders you see on draft animals. But while the blinder on a draft animal keeps it from getting spooked or distracted by objects in its peripheral vision, the blinder on a pen-raised game bird is meant to keep him from seeing clearly enough to maul his pen mates out of the frustration and anxiety that are the hallmarks of wild animals that are forced to live in tight confines.

---

*Some people's notions of challenge are even more difficult to comprehend. I recently read an editorial by a hunter who argued that other hunters rely on too many technologies. He bragged of wearing uninsulated XtraTuf boots in cold weather, his point being, I suppose, that insulated boots take away some of the challenge of being out in the cold. This struck me as odd, considering that XtraTuf boots are made with seamless laminates and triple-dipped in a neoprene coating that makes them impervious to water and resistant to ozone. How this is more authentic than a pair of leather boots with wool felt insulation is beyond me. It's interesting to note here that Otzi, the 5,300-year-old bow hunter found dead and mummified in the Italian Alps, was wearing insulated footwear.

When the birds were mature, Bill would sell them to wannabe "hunters" for nine or ten dollars each. When a client called, he'd go into his bird tent and collect the number of birds that the guy wanted to shoot. He'd put the birds in a cage and load the cage on his ATV and then drive them out into a field. One at a time, he'd pick out the birds and twirl them around with the windmill motion that Pete Townshend from the Who famously used to play his guitar. This would put the birds to sleep, or at least something resembling sleep. Then Bill would form a little hut out of field grass and tuck the bird into it. The timing of this was delicate. He wanted the birds to come to their senses soon enough that they'd fly away when the clients came along, but not so soon that they'd wander off in search of food before that happened.

When the clients came out, their activities certainly hinted at hunting. They would lead dogs and carry shotguns and shoot at edible birds that were flying through the air. But while game farm hunting does have these attributes of actual hunting, it lacks the beautiful essence of uncertainty that is to hunting what pan drippings are to gravy. The hunters' success did not come from the fact that they'd studied the species and learned its ways and scouted its habitat; instead it came because they paid some guy to raise the birds and then make sure that they were put out in a field where the hunters almost couldn't help but find them.

One day, Bill invited me to "hunt his place." This seemed like a strange choice of words for him to use. While Bill definitely advertised his business as "hunting," he in no way actually thought of it as hunting. For him, hunting was packing his horses twenty miles into the upper Greybull region of the Absaroka Mountains to chase mule deer, elk, and sometimes bighorn sheep on a landscape defined by craggy peaks, narrow trails, and big grizzlies. When I asked him about this, he explained that his season was winding down and that there were months' worth of runaway birds on the property that had either eluded his clients or escaped his nets.

At first I told him that I couldn't. With all due respect, I said, it ran contrary to my ethics. But then I got to thinking about it. I thought about how these bird species were not indigenous to this region or even to the continent; about how they'd probably never survive the winter; and about how, if they did, their presence on the land was at least as false a concept as hunting for them would be. I also considered how tasty they'd be. So I went out with Bill, shot a few birds, boned them out, and cooked them in a stir-fry. To this day I find myself thinking about the rightness and wrongness of that hunt. And I only mention it now so that I don't come across as overly cocky about the certitude of my own moral compass.

It's helpful to think of the ethics of hunting as a form of religion, in that most people's beliefs are influenced as much by where they were born as by what they've learned since leaving home. I grew up in an area where hunting deer over bait was the normal way of doing things. In late September, we'd sometimes drive up to a carrot processing facility near Grant, Michigan, where we could buy a pickup load of oversized and misshapen carrot rejects for five dollars. We'd then go to our hunting areas and shovel these carrots into a Duluth pack and lug them into the woods near the intersections of deer trails. Once a pile started getting hit by deer, we'd add more carrots and hang a tree stand in a nearby tree.

Hunting over bait, I spent an incalculable amount of cold and miserable hours without seeing a single deer. Sometimes the bow season would pass without my getting a shot at an animal except maybe a squirrel or grouse that passed beneath my tree. The limited number of deer that lived in my hunting area had adapted to the absurd abundance of bait piles in the woods and had learned to simply avoid them during daylight hours. After all, there were plenty of other foods for them to eat—such as the apples and corn in the orchards and fields that were often within a few hundred yards of our bait. So, by using a strategy that some might describe as cheating, or as taking away the challenge of the hunt, we were doing something that, in hindsight, had the effect of making deer hunting almost *too* challenging. Twentysomething years later, I no longer hunt over bait at all. My reasons for this are not based entirely on ethics. Instead I am not interested in using artificial bait because I am not interested in hunting animals that are doing artificial things. To go out and find a deer by solving the riddle of its natural patterns is far more enticing to me than finding a deer by interrupting those patterns. Baiting is not, in my opinion, a type of hunting that fosters an intelligent understanding of animals. But if you enjoy it, go ahead.

My impression of hunting animals with hounds was formed through an equally subjective and haphazard set of experiences. My introduction to this kind of hunting came when I was about eighteen years old and was invited to accompany a raccoon hunter whom we'll call Dave. It was the late summer training season, when you're allowed to exercise your coon dogs in the woods but you're not allowed to kill any raccoons. We went out at about 11 P.M. and turned the dogs out of the truck along a two-track. We then drove along with the dogs running out ahead of us, the way you see some lazy people exercise their pets. We hadn't gone a mile when the dogs struck a hot trail and bellowed their way down a slope and across a creek and into the darkness. Dave cut the truck's engine and we listened to the dogs. He could tell from the pitch and intensity of their barks that they had already brought the raccoon to bay. With headlamps we walked down the slope and across the creek and found the hounds scratching at a small oak. Up in the limbs were a female raccoon and several of her young cubs. Dave then explained to me that it wasn't good to pull the dogs away from the raccoons without killing one, because they might lose interest in hunting if they weren't properly rewarded. So he raised up a .22 pistol that I didn't even know he had and shot one of the raccoon cubs dead out of the tree. After that I told him I was done for the night, and I honestly figured that I wouldn't be hanging around any more houndsmen for at least a long time.*

But now, in the deserts of Arizona, I was not only hanging out

---

*Here I'd like to add another layer of subjectivity by admitting that my negative impression of this houndsman was influenced heavily by the fact that my brothers and I had owned three baby raccoons as pets. The first, a male named Critter, was given to us by a friend who had to remove a nest of raccoons from the attic of his parents' house. The second and third raccoons were male and female siblings that we named Poon and Tang. These came from the chimney of a woodstove at another friend's house. When my brother Danny went to get them, all he had to do was open the door of the stove and then reach inside to pick a couple out. We found raccoons to be the best pets in the world. I took them everywhere, even to drive-in movies. While their favorite foods were marshmallows, Mountain Dew, and venison jerky, they were also big fans of live seafood. We used to fill a kiddie pool with a few inches of water and then populate it with crayfish and chubs that we netted from our lake. Watching the raccoons chase around their dinner in the water was better entertainment than anything you'd find on TV. But the problem with raccoon ownership is that the animals begin to go wild and crazy when they're around seven months old. Critter got so territorial and aggressive that he'd attack you whenever you brought him a marshmallow. He somehow mistook the gesture of offering the treat as an attempt to steal it. He got to be so dangerous to be around that I had to drive him way back into the woods to release him into the wild. Some weeks later a buddy of mine pulled up in his truck and said he found my raccoon. When he opened the door, out rushed a raccoon that was certainly not Critter. The animal ran across the driveway, bit my dad on the leg, and then scurried up a tree. We then had to get a .22 and kill the raccoon in order to check it for rabies. Critter was never seen again, and we came to blame his maleness for his bad attitude. That's why we got both a male and a female the second time around. We figured that these two might become a breeding pair and then live contented lives in the house that we built for them and fastened to a white pine in the yard. This did not happen. Instead, the two raccoons slowly evolved into a sort of evil duo that would hang around outside the kitchen door and then fight their way inside whenever we opened it to enter or exit. My mom had to keep a landing net on hand in order to catch them and put them outside. One time, they discovered the grease drippings beneath a pig roaster at a neighbor's family reunion. They staked the roaster out, and then managed to thwart all attempts by the family to regain possession of their cooking pig. About a month later, when the acorns matured, they ascended an oak tree in our yard and spent almost a week up there, or at least a week's worth of days. I had no idea what they did at night. Then one morning they had simply vanished. We haven't seen them since.

with a pair of houndsmen; I was doing everything I could to help them. And, as I was learning, the pursuit of a lion is much more complicated than simply shooting an animal out of a tree. The real challenge was getting an animal into a tree in the first place. Doing that required finding something known in the parlance of lion hunters as an "overnight track." That means a lion track* that was made within the past eight or nine hours. When conditions are right—not too windy, not too dewy, not too rainy—a track of that vintage is likely to retain enough of the lion's residual odor for dogs to be able to pick up the scent and trail it. Yet despite the slaughter of calves that had occurred here the previous spring, and despite the recently killed deer that we had found, we had yet to locate a promising overnight track after days of searching for one.

Every day, Floyd and I would wake up well before sunrise. Joe would already be gone, having left so early in the morning that it was more like nighttime. Floyd and I would head into the desert with some predetermined landscape feature as our ultimate destination: mesas, rocky buttes, deeply incised canyons, high ridgelines, saddles, passes—all places where lions are likely to either hunt, sleep, or travel

---

*People often (and understandably) get confused by the various usages for the words *sign, track,* and *trail.* The definitions of these words do overlap, though each is also distinct. *Sign* refers to any evidence suggesting the presence, past or present, of animals. For instance, deer sign might include hoofprints, browsed leaves, droppings, frequently used paths, rubbed trees, tufts of hair on the barbs of barbed wire fences, and circular patches of scratched-up ground known as scrapes. As a noun, *track* refers to a physical paw print or hoofprint that's been stamped into the ground or snow by an animal's foot. In their verb forms, both *track* and *trail* refer to the act of following a single animal's route of travel by using any type of sign, be it tracks or otherwise. A "trail" can be either a physical path created by the frequent passage of animals or evidence of a single animal's passage—whether that evidence occurs in the form of tracks, odor, tufts of hair, blood, or anything else. While you might say that you tracked or trailed a deer by following its hoofprints, you would never say that you tracked a deer by following the blood that dripped from a wound. That would be trailing. Also, dogs don't track. That's because dogs are generally unconcerned with footprints and rely instead on odor, which is trailed.

through. Floyd is in his mid-fifties and his appearance brings to mind Robert Redford when the actor was about that same age. He's part owner of *Western Hunter* and *Elk Hunter* magazines, and full owner of Outdoorsmans, an iconic Phoenix sporting goods store that specializes in high-end European-made optics as well as Outdoorsmans' own line of American-made backpack and tripod systems. His line of work allows him to think of chasing lions as a business-related activity, which means he can hunt as much as he wants to without having to feel guilty about it. Some years ago, he and his girlfriend owned and operated an aerial photography company. This required Floyd to buy a helicopter. "I learned to fly a helicopter in a month," he told me. "Meanwhile I've been hunting lions for twenty years and I'm still learning stuff. Lion hunting is the hardest thing I've ever done."

At least on this hunt, Floyd mostly preferred to look for overnight tracks without the assistance of his dogs. For one thing, he didn't want them to get tired out before it was time to actually chase a lion. For another thing, the passage of all those dogs' paws has the potential to disturb the delicate evidence that a lion might leave while traveling over a portion of the earth's surface that is covered predominately in rock, cactus, and grass—surfaces that do not readily collect the tracks of a passing animal. Floyd calls himself a "bare-ground lion hunter," a description that differentiates him from guys who hunt colder and wetter regions with predictable and frequent dosages of snow—the world's most track-friendly substance. While a big lion can weigh up to 150 pounds and can kill an elk weighing four times as much, they seem to walk about as gently as a balloon hitting the ground. The only place that they'll leave a track is in the sand, and around here sand occurs primarily in the same places—creek beds, game trails—that attract a lot of competing traffic from mule deer, javelina, cattle, quail, bobcats, coyotes, bighorn sheep—and dogs if you let them run out ahead of you.

Floyd spends so much time studying the ground for lion tracks that it's begun to affect his posture. His natural stance has his eyes staring at the ground directly ahead of his boots. He's trained himself to tune out everything on the ground except for the tracks of lions. On average these measure about three-and-a-half inches from front to back and side to side. Perfect, complete lion tracks are far less common than imperfect, partial lion tracks. You might just see the imprint of a few toes in the sand, or the outline of a track that's interrupted by a flat piece of rock. The important part of a lion track, the part that eliminates imposters, is the trailing edge of the heel pad. It leaves an impression in the sand that looks like the bottom of these letters put together: UUU.*

When we were out looking for tracks, Floyd and I had many conversations that went like this:

"Here's something interesting," I'd say. "This has got to be a lion. It looks a little like a dog, but it's a lot rounder. You should check it out."

"Can you see the heel pad?" Floyd would ask.

"No," I'd say.

"Look for another one," he'd say.

Then, finally, it happened. After five long days of doing little but walking and looking for tracks, I found what we were searching for. It was below a large butte, in a dry creek bed where a few boulders funneled the animal traffic into a narrow gap. "Here you go," I called out to Floyd. "Here's a heel pad, surer than hell."

Floyd walked over to have a look. His face registered a moment of interest, but then his enthusiasm waned. "Looks to me like a coyote track where he spun around in the sand. So it looks bigger than nor-

---

*The tracks of other native North American cats, including bobcats, lynx, and jaguars, also have three-lobed heel pads. An exception to this is the ocelot, which has only two lobes.

mal," he said. "Then a javelina stepped on the back of it. That's what gives it that lobed look. And notice how you don't see any more good tracks ahead of it or behind it. Just coyote and javelina. Keep in mind," he went on, "anything can make a lion track once. It takes a lion to do it twice. You find me two good tracks with lobed pads, and then you've got something worth looking at."

While I was disappointed by our inability to find a good lion track, I was hardly surprised. Prior to my visit to Arizona I had had only three physical encounters with wild mountain lions.* Each of those encounters reinforced my notion of the animal as a secretive and elusive creature. The first encounter stands out in my mind most visibly. It happened near Clearwater Lake, in Montana's Swan Mountains, just after I moved out West. That night I'd been fly-fishing for cutthroat trout and I stayed on the water until a little past dark. When I was done, I hiked three-quarters of a mile through the woods back to where my van was parked on a forest service road. It was pitch-black by the time I began the long and bumpy drive out toward Highway 83. About halfway along, I came to a place where the forest service road had been cut into the side of a steep hillside. I rounded a corner and there was a gang of mule deer does and fawns all bunched up in the middle of the road. When I got close, they ran to the right and struggled up the steeply pitched hillside in a whirl of hooves and falling rocks.

Just as this was happening, I caught in my side-view mirror a sudden flash of movement in the halo of the brake lights. I shoved the shifter upward into reverse, so that the van's backup lights would come on, and then I stuck my head out the window to look. There it was, standing within inches of the rear bumper: the first mountain

---

*Saying you saw a mountain lion in a zoo is like saying you met George Washington at a wax museum. In all, these three sightings amounted to about thirty seconds of lion-viewing time.

lion I ever saw. He spun himself in a turn that seemed like wine swirling in a glass. With that, the lion vanished into the dark.

Over the next few weeks, I thought about that mountain lion far
more than I've ever thought about any single living creature besides a
dog named Duchess that my family owned for about thirteen years. I
did a fair bit of thinking about what the lion was doing before I interrupted its hunt that night. But I did a lot more thinking about what it
did afterward. To the north of where I saw the cat was the largest tract
of contiguous wilderness in the lower forty-eight. I was baffled by the
mystery of that lion amid all that country. What did it do over the
next few days? Where did it hunt? What did it eat? Where did it sleep?
How did it react to the world that it encountered? Where did it *go*?

As I pondered these questions and researched the answers, I realized that the people with the most sophisticated understanding of
mountain lions were the men and women who hunted them with
hounds. By following their hounds as they track a lion, houndsmen
get to literally walk in the trail of their quarry. They see where the lion
hunts; they see where the lion eats; they see where the lion sleeps.
They experience the land on the terms of the lion. They know where
the lion *goes*.

The lion hunter is also, I found out, one of the most hated types
of hunters in the country. If you think of the conflict between hunters
and anti-hunters as a long-term war, the right to hunt lions with
hounds is the current frontline battlefield in many western states.
This would have been unforeseeable just a hundred years ago, when it
was common practice for states to offer bounties on mountain lions
because of the cat's tendency to prey on livestock. In Arizona, killing
a lion would earn you fifty dollars. In the 1960s and '70s, western
states began to recognize mountain lions as an important part of the
ecosystem, and also as a species of interest to big-game hunters. Most
states reclassified lions as a game species and made it necessary for

hunters to buy a legal hunting license and a mountain lion permit in order to kill one.

There are several ways to hunt lions. You can try to attract them with a predator call, which typically mimics the sounds of wounded deer or rabbits. Or you can hang around in good lion country, hoping that one of the cats happens to come along. But by far the most effective way to hunt mountain lions is through the use of dogs. In Montana, 89 percent of lion hunters use dogs. In Wyoming, it's 90 percent. Over the last twenty-five years, 65 percent of all lions harvested by hunters in Arizona were killed with the help of dogs.

Anti-hunters have long recognized the importance of dogs in hunting lions. I believe that the more organized factions of anti-hunters camouflage their opposition to hunting in general as a more specific opposition to hunting lions with dogs. It allows them to wage small-scale legal battles against the broader spectrum of hunting without having to conquer the issue head-on. Some of these battles have proved winnable, as it's easy to convince people who have never once hunted or laid eyes on a wild lion that hunting animals with dogs is somehow a perverse activity. In 1994, Oregon voters passed an initiative that banned hunting lions with dogs, though hunting lions by other means remains legal. The same thing is true in Washington and South Dakota: Hunt lions? Yes. With dogs? No. If you're puzzled about how such laws could ever come into existence, consider the results of a 2001 poll of Arizona residents. While only 29 percent of those polled indicated that hunting should be banned outright, 62 percent indicated that the use of hounds to hunt lions should be illegal.

To be perfectly honest, I was inspired by my personal lion experience to reconsider my own suspicions about the practice of hunting them with hounds. I wanted to see one of the animals up close, and to experience the thrill of eating its flesh, and the only realistic way for me to do this was to join up with some houndsmen and head into the hills in search of a track. If we got one into a tree and I didn't like the way it felt, I could always walk away without killing it.

While we were hunting lions, Floyd's partner, Joe, slept in the back of his pickup on a pad of carpet. He kept his dogs tethered outside of the truck scattered apart so that they didn't fight or get tangled up. When he got up, at 3 A.M., he would pull on a pair of faded Levi's, Danner hunting boots, and one of Floyd's Outdoorsmans backpacks, and then he would unclip the pack of hounds and they would take off together into the darkness. They would cover several miles before it got light out, and then another six or seven miles after daybreak. This was an impressive bit of walking for a man who'd retired from the concrete-laying business with past injuries including but not limited to a shattered sternum (concrete finisher), a gnawed leg (mountain lion), and a gunshot wound (sustained after dropping a .357 revolver in such a way that the hammer hit the concrete and discharged a round). As Joe walked, he would use a headlamp to study the earth in front of him for tracks. His dogs would range out to the sides and ahead of his line of travel with their noses to the ground. By their specific barks, he could tell whether they were detecting the recent passage of a lion.

He spent five whole days this way, without any significant strokes of luck. Then, on our last day of hunting, Floyd and I were getting ready to leave camp when we heard a cacophony of bellows coming from Joe's dogs high on the mountain above us. It sounded like someone torturing a gang of opera singers. Even from a great distance, Floyd knew exactly what Joe's dogs were saying. "That dog you hear there, with the low bellow, he doesn't make noise on an old lion trail.

He's too old and wise for that. He only makes noise on a good over-night track."

We studied the mountainside where the barking was coming from and soon spotted the flickers of light from Joe's headlamp. He was moving quickly across the face of the mountain. There was a notch in the skyline that marked the entrance to a canyon, and soon Joe's light disappeared into that notch. The sounds from the dogs' barking began to fade as the distance increased. Joe's voice then came over the walkie-talkie. He implored Floyd to cut loose some of his dogs.

"Have you seen a track yet?" asked Floyd. "Any idea what way the lion's going? Is it a tom?"

"No tracks yet," said Joe. "But they're really moving the trail. Just get some dogs loose and get them up here."

Floyd unleashed six of his own dogs, who immediately headed uphill toward the source of the barking. Floyd then turned to me and said, "We better get moving."

The canyon that Joe and the dogs entered described a long arc, Floyd explained. He figured that we might catch up with them by following a neighboring canyon through a straighter route. We headed across a sage patch, past some saguaro cactuses, and then into the mouth of the canyon. The daylight grew as we made our way into the dry brown mountains. As we walked, Floyd explained the trouble of chasing a lion that the dogs could smell but that you haven't seen a track from. While the dogs can certainly tell that a lion has passed through, they are not able to determine which direction it is traveling. This can lead to obvious and considerable confusion. As Floyd put it, "there's a fifty-fifty chance that the dogs are taking you in the wrong direction."

After a mile of walking we still hadn't heard the dogs and we couldn't tell where Joe had gone. We were unable to reach him on the walkie-talkie, as the deeply cut topography interfered with the transmissions. We traveled another mile and then left the canyon bottom and started walking uphill toward a ridgeline. When we got up there, we still couldn't hear anything. I noticed a high, thumb-shaped spire of rock that rose out of the mountains like a city skyscraper rising above buildings half its height. I commented to Floyd that the lion was probably headed that way, or at least that's where I'd head if I were being chased and wanted to elude my pursuers. Floyd replied that the lion still didn't know it was being chased. He'd been here hours earlier and was probably off sleeping somewhere, oblivious to our presence in the world.

We pressed on. Hours went by, and the day passed into the afternoon. As it would turn out, the lion had indeed headed toward the thumb-shaped spire of rock—whether or not he knew he was being followed. Later, Floyd and I would finally meet up with Joe near its base. By then the dogs would have lost the lion's trail, and they'd be too exhausted to follow it even if they hadn't. We would find them lolling around on a jumble of rocks. Now and then, one of the dogs would lick a certain rock and bellow, its saliva having released some trace of the lion's odor. Then it would head off in some direction or another, making a ruckus. I would get excited all over again, thinking that I might still get my chance to see a lion up close. But each time, the dog would return, having lost interest in what was becoming an increasingly cold trail. Finally Joe and Floyd suggested that we start the long walk back toward camp. We all had to be somewhere the next day. I walked away in silence, disappointed that I was unable to learn whether it was challenging to shoot a lion out of a tree. Getting to that final moment of truth had been, quite simply, too challenging.

||||||||||||||||||||||||||||||||||||||||||||||||||||||||||||||||||||||||||||||||||||||||||||||||||||||||||||||

Tasting Notes: Mountain Lion

I've eaten at least as many mountain lions as I've seen in the wild, which is not something I can say about any other species of North American mammal. The first time I tried it was in Montana, when a six-inch section of a lion's loin, or backstrap, found its way into my home through a friend of a friend who shot it in the Bitterroot Mountains. At first I was a little bit reluctant to cook it, for three main reasons: 1) It seemed like a form of betrayal to be eating a fellow carnivore whose preferred foods—deer and elk—were exactly the same as my own; 2) the meat had a pale, veal-like color that matched the lurid descriptions of human flesh that I've encountered while reading historical accounts of the cannibalistic Indian tribes of the Great Lakes region; and 3) the meat forced me to conjure the mental image of gutting a mountain lion and finding a bellyful of raw, freshly chewed venison rather than the usual shredded vegetation that you find in the paunch of most big-game animals. The idea of a lion's stomach led me to have visions of what my own stomach might look like after a big meal of meat—and if there's one idea that can wreck a person's appetite, it's the thought of having your stomach spilled out for viewing.

We all know the saying about how curiosity kills the cat; well, curiosity also gets the cat eaten. After a day or two of pondering the loin, I decided to at least cook the thing in order to see what happened. I used the same preparation that I like to use on wild boar loin: sprinkle it with Montreal seasoning, sear it on all sides in a pan, and then roast it in an oven. (Mountain lions are carriers of *Trichinella spiralis,* so you want to cook it to a high temperature.) When I pulled the meat out, it looked and smelled so much like pork that I couldn't help but slice off an eighth of an inch and pop it into my mouth. I was fully prepared to spit it back out again, but instead I had another slice. In addition to appearance, it resembled wild boar in both texture and flavor. In fact, I'm pretty sure you could do a double-blind taste test between the loins of a mountain lion and a wild boar and you'd stump 90 percent of the participants.

The legs of a mountain lion are a different story. I found this out about a year after I tasted my first piece of lion meat. An ex-girlfriend, who grew up in Wyoming, was visiting her family when she happened to be standing in line behind a guy in a hardware store who was buying a mountain lion hunting permit. She interrupted the guy to ask what he was planning on doing with all that lion meat, figuring, correctly, that he didn't have any plans for the meat whatsoever. She gave him her phone number on a scrap of paper. A week later he called to say that he had a quartered-out cougar wrapped in plastic garbage bags and ready to be picked up. We thawed a rear ham as soon as she returned to Montana. I removed the femur and shinbone, rubbed it inside and out with seasoning, and baked it in the oven like a fresh pork ham. It came out so tough that I was inspired to think of ways in which it might be put to use in industrial or automotive applications.

The remainder of the lion, minus the backstraps, was still in my freezer that spring when I happened to turn up at the Rock Creek Lodge. This bar sits at the confluence of Rock Creek and the Clark Fork River, about twenty miles east of Missoula, Montana. It's regionally famous for its annual Testicle Festival, a liquor-fueled carnival where ranchers, hippies, loggers, bikers, and college kids get together in September in order to get drunk, shed clothes, dance, and occasionally fight, all in the name of eating deep-fried Rocky Mountain oysters. But on this day the Testicle Festival was still a half year away, and the bar was mostly empty except for a plastic bag of hamburger buns and an electric roasting pan that was filled with chipped meat and a tangy barbecue sauce. I was well into my third sandwich—it was free, after all—when the owner of the place came out and asked how I liked the cougar meat. "I like it a lot," I told him.

"Bet you didn't know what it was," he said.

"You're right."

He explained that his buddy down the road was a professional mountain lion hunting guide, but that the man's clients never wanted to bring any of the meat home except for the backstraps. "I take as much as I can get," he said. "Simmer the quarters in water until the meat's falling off the bone, and then chunk it all up and make some sauce. It's better than pork once you get it tender, if you ask me." When I left the bar, the man called after me to announce a slogan that he'd just thought of: "Rock Creek Lodge: Balls in the fall, pussy in the spring!"

I'm not sure how far he made it with his advertising plan, but I got a lot of mileage out of his recipe. I spent the next couple of months making batch after batch of barbecued cougar, and even hosted a large mountain lion party where a couple dozen friends feasted on the sandwiches. They were all delighted by the experience. Later that night, I figured that there were more bellyfuls of lion meat running around my Missoula neighborhood than at any other time during the past hundred years at least. For whatever reason, the image of all those meat-packed stomachs did not bother me. The lion had made me stronger.

||||||||||||||||||||||||||||||||||||||||||||||||||||||||||||||||||||||||||||||||||||||||||||||||||||

CHAPTER ELEVEN

The Remains

★

DANNY AND I are on a mountain that has no name. It rises up from the water directly behind our shack on Prince of Wales Island, up to an elevation of about two thousand feet. No roads, no landing strips for bush planes. To get up here you have to climb. We arrived last night and pitched our tent in a storm. This morning we crawled out into the rain and hunted all day before killing two blacktail deer near the peak. The animals died out of sight of each other, and Danny and I split up so that we could both butcher our own. It took me about thirty minutes to skin the carcass and cut it into transportable pieces. Now, with the job done, I'm leaving behind a tangled pile of ivory-white bones. Also a purplish mound of internal organs. I cut away the animal's antlers and skullcap with a bone saw, leaving the brain exposed but perfectly intact. The sight of the remains might appear gruesome to some, but to me it seems wholesome, almost appetizing. This is what remains after meat gets made. It also seems appetizing to the raven that is already riding a thermal above me while it croaks news of the kill. As I pull on the backpack full of meat, I consider how to bid a proper farewell to a butchered carcass. It might seem strange to thank an animal that you just killed, as it likely did everything in its power to avoid giving you the gift of its life. Yet doing so is the only thing that seems proper. How else do you reconcile your happiness over an animal's death with your sense of reverence for its life?

Danny and I know it will be difficult and slow work to get down the mountain, so we decide to spend another night up here so that we don't get stuck mid-slope in the dark. We build a large fire on an exposed rock, and then experience the odd sensation of having our clothes dry from the heat at the same time that they get wet from the rain. At a point when it seems that the battle has reached a stalemate of general dampness, we strip down and leave our wet outer layers in the tent's vestibule and then slither into the warmth of our bags.

It's still raining in the morning when we start picking our way down the mountain. We decide on a route that might be quicker and more direct than the one we took on the way up and soon realize our mistake. We hit the precipice of a nearly vertical thirty-foot cliff of mud-covered rock. There are two ways to handle the situation. Either go back up and then try another route, or lower our packs on a climbing rope and rappel down behind them. We choose the latter, and then revel in the thrill of trusting our lives to a length of line and the strength of our hands.

The legs and arms of our clothes are covered with mud by the time we pick up our packs and resume walking. The lower we go, the thicker the alders get. But then they begin to peter out when we enter an area of old-growth forest that deprives the understory of light. The cedars here are so big that two people can't reach around them. There are some ferns, too, and their wet leaves wash the mud away from our clothes and leave us as soaked as if we'd showered fully dressed. My hands are numb with cold, and a pinched nerve in my shoulder emits a sharp and nagging pain from the weight of my meat and gear. I think of the hardships that I've endured in order to live in a way that makes sense to me. Cold, hunger, thirst, labor, exhaustion, loneliness, and fear are just a few things from a long list that come to mind. Is it strange, I wonder, to willfully suffer for one's food at a time when it's completely unnecessary to do so? As we walk, I'm reminded of a quote from the writer Thomas K. Whipple:

> All America lies at the end of the wilderness road, and our past is not a dead past, but still lives in us. Our forefathers had civilization inside themselves, the wild outside. We live in the civilization they created, but within us the wilderness still lingers. What they dreamed, we live, and what they lived, we dream.

Yet a few of us try to dream *and* live the wilderness. Of course, we cannot live it in the same way that our forefathers did. We cannot share their vicious disregard for the future of wild places. We cannot share their belief that the American wilderness is infinite in its ability to produce wild animals. My hero Daniel Boone learned this lesson in his own heartbreaking way. His passage through the Cumberland Gap and down into the Kentucky wilderness has been treated by historians as a Moses-like moment in which he led his people to the promised land. But in actuality, Boone came to lament his actions. The settlers who followed him chopped down the canebrakes, plowed up the grasslands, trapped out the beaver, poisoned off the panthers and wolves, and shot out the buffalo, elk, deer, bear, and turkey.

Luckily for Boone, he had a way out: the ever-expanding western frontier. From Kentucky he moved to the next wild west of Missouri, and then on to the next wild west of the Great Plains. In his eighties, he may have gone as far as Montana's Yellowstone River. Because he could always look ahead to fresh ground, he had the luxury of turning his back on the spoiled land that he left behind. Today, hunters do not have that luxury. We've had to become frontiersmen of a different breed: The ground and the animals that we leave behind are the same ones that we'll be returning to tomorrow and the day after.

The pitch of the mountain tapers off as Danny and I descend. Soon we're on a gradually sloping bench of land that has been made nearly impassable by fallen timber. We climb over some logs and under others, and just when it seems we'll never break free of the downed timber, we see a rising column of smoke. It's coming from the chimney of our neighbors' place, which sits across the creek from our own. Ron and Joan are two of the six people who live year-round on this remote cove that is accessible only by air or water. They are probably sitting down to dinner now, eating something that Ron killed with his own hands. The sight of the smoke fills me with both excitement and disappointment. The excitement comes from the thought of being out of the wild and safe from danger. The disappointment comes from the exact same thing.

I pitched in with Matt and Danny and another friend to buy our shack in 2004. At the time, my brothers and I were in that brief period of life when we had money but no spouses to tell us how to spend it. The shack is a lopsided and shoe-box-shaped structure that sits on tilted pilings over the tide line. It is completely off the grid. We get our water from a gravity-fed hose dunked into the creek that comes off the mountain behind the house and flows beneath the front right corner of the deck. For the most part, phones do not get a signal. We heat the shack and our hot tub—a large livestock watering tank—with wood-burning stoves. Instead of a flush toilet there's a hole in the ground and a bucket of lime. Mink drag their catch into the workshop and leave the bones and scales where they fall. Old-growth spruce and hemlock lean menacingly over everything we own—including the three chain saws, three outboard engines, one skiff, dozens of rusted oil drums, and hundreds of even rustier tools that the previous owner abandoned when he walked away from the place and never returned.

It was near this shack that my wife, Katie, witnessed her first kill. It happened just after Danny got married out here, during a celebration that was interrupted when a black bear sow and her two cubs came strolling through. Most of our friends and family left the next day, but Katie and I stayed for a while to hang out with Danny and his new bride, Corrina. Danny wanted to get a deer that he could bring home, so one morning we loaded up our skiff with a rifle and some gear in order to go hunting. I asked Katie to come along. She was a little bit reluctant to watch a deer get killed, so she politely declined. I kept after her about it and convinced her that whatever deer we encountered would be far away and obscured by brush and she wouldn't even see it until it was dead.

We landed the skiff at a creek mouth where you could walk up the channel toward a large grass flat that often had some deer hanging around. We were just approaching the edge of the flat when three deer came trotting right down the stream toward us. I didn't know if they'd been spooked by a wolf or a bear or what, but they were moving quickly and hardly paying attention to what was ahead of them. We hunkered near some boulders and waited. The deer didn't slow down until they were so close that I could see their eyelashes. One of them had a set of spike antlers, which meant it was a legal buck. I was hoping that Danny would have some sympathy for Katie and not shoot the deer so close to her. But he probably never even considered the situation that it would put me in, and he shot it through the brisket. The deer took about ten jumps and then piled up, stone dead.

Tears had already begun to fall across Katie's cheeks when I turned to look at her. She looked back at me as though I was brutal and distant. I hadn't been the one who pulled the trigger, but that distinction did not matter to her. As we stared at each other, I knew that I was seeing across a divide of time that is thousands of years wide. It was the chasm that separates our hunting ancestors from their civilized progeny. The chasm that separates Esau from Jacob. Probably wisely, I refrained from articulating this to Katie. Instead, Danny and I went over to gut the animal and drag it back to the boat. As we worked, I knew that the space between Katie and me would either grow or shrink, depending on her eventual interpretation of what she saw.

Later that night, lying scrunched in our bunk, she explained that the initial shock of witnessing the deer's death was stunning to her. But after pondering it for a while, she realized that there was nothing brutal or dishonest about what had happened. The deer was going about its usual routine in its natural habitat; it was part of a healthy and stable population, managed for longevity; it was never held captive or made to be afraid; and its death came from a knowledgeable predator who would utilize its body with respect. The next day she caught her first halibut, and then she became pregnant within a week. Months later, I would find great pleasure lying in bed with the small of my back pressed against the swell of her growing belly as she lay on her side. I could feel the baby slithering and probing. I imagined that my back was the earth, and my son was a hunter crawling upon its surface while stalking his prey.

Danny and I unload the backpacks full of deer meat on the deck of our open-air workshop. We remove eight legs, four loins, two hearts and livers, plus sacks of assorted boneless cuts. We pick off the stray pieces of hair and the little bits of lichen and blueberry leaves that inevitably collect on meat in the field. Once it's clean, we trim away the sinew and silver skin and cut the large pieces into meal-sized portions. When we're done we have a gorgeous pile of meat, good enough to be eaten raw. It's a quantity that could keep us fed for weeks. Behind us, on the mountain, are plenty more deer. In front of us, an ocean full of shrimp, crab, salmon, and halibut. Staring at the bounty around me, it is easy to envision a world just like this: nothing but the wilderness, civilization gone, me alone to hunt the animals and eat them. No guidance from the law, no interference. This is a dream that I have entertained my entire life. It is the dream of the modern hunter, and it has been essential to my existence. Lately, though, it's been occurring to me that I never once bothered to define the things that might turn such a dream into reality. The list might include disease, war, and ecological collapse. I realize that each version is a nightmare too horrible to contemplate, let alone fantasize.

Earlier, I wrote of the things that I've suffered while in pursuit of a lifestyle that makes sense to me. Things such as cold, hunger, loneliness, and fear. What I failed to mention are the ways in which I've been blessed through that same pursuit. While hunting, I've cried at the beauty of mountains covered in snow. I've learned to own up to my past mistakes, to admit them freely, and then to behave better the next time around. I've learned to see the earth as a thing that breathes and writhes and brings forth life. I see these revelations as a form of grace and art, as beautiful as the things we humans attempt to capture through music, dance, and poetry. And as I've become aware of this, it has become increasingly difficult for me to see hunting as altogether outside of civilization. Maybe stalking the woods is as vital to the human condition as playing music or putting words to paper. Maybe hunting has as much of a claim on our civilized selves as anything else. After all, the earliest forms of representational art reflect hunters and prey. While the arts were making us spiritually viable, hunting did the heavy lifting of not only keeping us alive, but inspiring us. To abhor hunting is to hate the place from which you came, which is akin to hating yourself in some distant, abstract way.

Of course, we have other attributes that are as old as art and hunting, and just as pervasive. Human violence stands out among these. I'm reminded of this reality when I head home from my shack and arrive at an airport in a city a thousand miles away and on a different coast. I go to the luggage carousel to collect my backpack and two coolers packed full of frozen venison. From there I go to baggage services to retrieve my rifle. I am prepared for a hassle. I have in hand my driver's license and my New York City shotgun/rifle permit, a costly and onerous piece of plastic that says I'm of sound enough mind to bring a high-powered long-range rifle into a city of eight million people. I hand the woman the driver's license and she nods toward where the case is set against the wall. I pick it up and walk out, thankful that I don't have to deal with the police. I lay the case across the top of the coolers on my cart and push it out through the automatic glass doors.

Outside, I take my place in the taxi line. I notice from a couple of people's suspicious glances that they know a gun case when they see one. They give me uneasy looks, as if to ask, "What are you doing here? Why are you among us?" It bothers me to think that a pragmatic food-acquisition tool should carry the connotations of violence, though the parallels between the two cannot be denied. Each involves weapons, bloodshed, and taking possession of something that one covets through violence. But the difference between the two is fundamental enough to make the similarities irrelevant. War is an act of hate, while hunting is an act of love. The warrior does not decorate his home with beautiful images of his enemy; he does not donate money to the preservation of his enemy's habitat; he does not manage his own property with a goal of attracting his enemy for viewing; he does not obey a code of conduct meant not only to stabilize his enemy's numbers but to increase them.

———

My wife and son are asleep in the bedroom when I get home. Katie is in our bed, and Jim's in a crib that sits behind a curtain that we strung between the walls in order to give him his own private space. Next to his crib is the door to a large closet that houses my chest freezer. Early tomorrow morning, when my son wakes up, I'll be able to transfer my new supply of wild meat into the freezer. Then I'll tally up what I've brought, how many months' worth of food I've collected, and my wife will add the items to a spreadsheet that I keep pinned to a corkboard in the kitchen. While I'd like to thaw out a celebratory piece of the meat now, for tomorrow's dinner, I try to honor a freezer-management policy of last in, last out. We'll have to finish a few other animals before we start in on the deer. By then, Jim will be old enough to have his first pieces of meat. I will fry him a piece of the venison and mash it into a paste along with some boiled yam in a mortar and pestle. I will then lean over and present it to him on a small spoon. He will eat it without hesitation, like something he was born to do.

It's an October night, cold enough that I can put the coolers out in the vegetable garden and the meat will stay frozen until dawn. I open the back door and carry them outside. I go back inside and sit on the couch. Around me are a few skulls and hides and sets of horns and antlers. They are reminders of a hunting life. Staring at them, I remember the set of antlers that I swaddled in clothes and packed into my backpack. I open my backpack up and pull them out. There is still a little flesh on the skullcap. I will clean it later, by boiling the bone and scraping it clean. I'm thinking that I might hang the antlers in the kitchen, in a place where it will make a good rack for cooking utensils. That way, the deer will continue to help me eat long after its flesh has been consumed.

But for now, I take the antlers outside and hang them on a section of fence. I want to put them where they can be seen from the living room window. That way, when it's raining and we can't play outside,

I can hold my son, Jim, on my hip and we can look out at them while I tell him the story of where the antlers came from, and what happened that day on the mountain. I go back inside and check the window to make sure they're in a good place. I can see the light of the city. The blackened shadows of buildings. Somewhere in the distance, I can hear the sounds of sirens. Out there is everything that civilization has wrought, and reminders of everything that it lost in the process. Set against it, from my perspective, the deer's antlers stand out brightly. They are like a flag rising defiantly above the smoke of an embattled and surrounded stronghold. They are a reminder to anyone who sees them: There are hunters here, within us.

Acknowledgments

A proper acknowledgment page might just say "Thanks to everyone I know," since I do a poor job of shielding my friends, family, and colleagues from the particular brand of turmoil that goes hand-in-hand with completing a book. But my obligations are deep enough to require some specificity, so here goes: Thanks to Joe Caterini, Chris Collins, and Lydia Tenaglia at Zero Point Zero Productions for taking me in. Thanks also to their beautifully reckless and die-hard producers and crew, especially Jared Andrukanis, Nick Brigden, Helen Cho, Dan Doty, and Morgan Fallon. I'm proud to have traveled with you guys, and I look forward to more.

Thanks to Bobby Hottensen and Tom Tiberio for their help with various research questions that I encountered while writing this book. Other valuable pieces of information, insight, and recollection came from Adam Bump and Russ Mason of the Michigan Department of Natural Resources, Dan Flores of the University of Montana, and Matt Carlson, Don Clifford, Parker Dozhier, Katie Finch, Rosemary Johnson, Daniel Rinella, Matthew Rinella, the late Frank Rinella, and Julie Stewart.

For the best hunting and fishing memories that a guy could ask for, I have to thank Craig Christensen, Al Cole, Ronny Boehme, Matt Drost, Eugene Groters, Eric Kern, Matt Moisan, Andrew (Pooder) Radzialowski, and Danny and Matt Rinella (once again). Plus Matt's pack llamas, especially Timmy and Haggy.

Thanks to Jim Harrison, a man I've never actually met but who changed my life for the better. Thanks to my agent (and buddy) Marc Gerald, who's provided me with unwavering encouragement and guidance and promptly answered emails for the past eight years. Thanks to my editor and publisher, Cindy Spiegel at Spiegel & Grau, one of my favorite people in the world and one of very few publishers with the wherewithal to bag a western cottontail rabbit with a .22 rifle. Thanks also to Julie Grau, Hana Landes, and the other great folks at both Spiegel & Grau and Random House.

Finally, I'd like to thank my beautiful wife for generally tolerating a freezer full of game meat in our closet, shotguns and rifles in our bedroom, and various bloody animal parts in our refrigerator. Even when she does bitch about it, she has the generosity and grace to do it in a way that's funny.

Research Notes and Suggestions
for Further Reading

My understanding of arctic and subarctic hunters and wildlife was enhanced by *Make Prayers to the Raven, Hunters of the Northern Forest*, and *Hunters of the Northern Ice*, by Richard K. Nelson; *A Naturalist's Guide to the Arctic*, by E. C. Pielou; *Interior & Northern Alaska: A Natural History*, by Ronald L. Smith; and *My Life with the Eskimo*, by Vilhjalmur Stefansson.

My understanding of human evolution and migration was influenced by *First Peoples in a New World*, by David J. Meltzer; *The Seven Daughters of Eve*, by Bryan Sykes; *Before the Dawn*, by Nicholas Wade; and *The Journey of Man*, by Spencer Wells. A great source for information about the hunting methods and belief systems of aboriginal African hunters can be found in the works of Laurens van der Post, particularly *The Lost World of the Kalahari* and *The Heart of the Hunter*.

There are many great books about Daniel Boone, some of them outrageous and some of them thorough and grounded. I have read most of them, and the best and most contemporary examination of the man and the legend is *Boone: A Biography*, by Robert Morgan. Another great source of information about Boone and his era is the writing of historian Ted Franklin Belue, particularly *The Hunters of Kentucky*.

Good contemporary writing about the mountain men of the

Rockies is woefully lacking, in my opinion. However, I have found some fascinating anecdotes and passages about these men in *Jim Bridger*, by J. Cecil Alter; *Give Your Heart to the Hawks*, by Win Blevins; *The Mountain Men*, by George Laycock; *Journal of a Trapper*, by Osborne Russell; and *Tales of the Mountain Men*, by Lamar Underwood.

Index

Page numbers in *italics* indicate photographs.